Della Raye

Della Raye
A Girl Who Grew Up in Hell
and
Emerged Whole

Gary Penley

PELICAN PUBLISHING COMPANY
Gretna 2002

The word "Pelican" and the depiction of a pelican are trademarks of Pelican Publishing Company, Inc., and are registered in the U.S. Patent and Trademark Office.

Library of Congress Cataloging-in-Publication Data

Penley, Gary, 1941-
    Della Raye : a girl who grew up in hell and emerged
    whole / Gary Penley.
        p. cm.
    ISBN 1-56554-944-9
    1. Rogers, Della Raye, 1924- 2. Mental retardation facilities
patients—Alabama—Biography. 3. Partlow State School
and Hospital—History. 4.
Eugenics—United States—History. I. Title.

RC570.5.U6 P464 2002
362.3'092—dc21
    [B]

                                            2001036773

Note: The names of some characters in this story have been changed for reasons of privacy.

Photos provided courtesy of Della Raye Rogers Hughes

Printed in the United States of America
Published by Pelican Publishing Company, Inc.
1000 Burmaster Street, Gretna, Louisiana 70053

To Massie, an angel in bedlam

"Few tragedies can be more extensive than the stunting of life, few injustices deeper than the denial of an opportunity to strive or even to hope, by a limit imposed from without, but falsely identified as lying within."

—Stephen Jay Gould, *The Mismeasure of Man*

Contents

Preface

Rarely does a person exist who can endure years of unspeakable abuse, emotional neglect, and mental deprivation yet remain unbroken by the experience. Rarer still is one with the courage to confront her demons and the depth of character to forgive her tormentors.

Wrongly imprisoned in a mental institution in the Depression-ridden South for twenty years—from age four to twenty-four—Della Raye grew up in Hell and emerged whole, but could not bear to speak of her childhood for decades thereafter. But the unyielding courage and faith that enabled her to endure the unspeakable never faltered. After fifty years the lady gathered up a lifetime of hidden memories and carried them out of the darkness into the sunlight.

Della Raye enjoys life as a vigorous seventy-something now; a friendly face, ready smile, and gaily flowered dress greet the world. The shelves of her tidy home are filled with hundreds of books, its walls adorned with family pictures, prayers, and mementos of a well-spent life. In an amiable patter of non-stop conversation, a delightful laugh escapes her merry face and a childlike sparkle dances in her eyes. "I'll tell you something funny!" she says. And it always is.

Della Raye did more than survive—she freed her own soul from bitterness. Only true courage can combat such an ordeal, and when the battle is done, only true forgiveness can make one whole again.

Acknowledgments

I wish to express my gratitude to Dr. Edward Larson, Professor of History and Law, University of Georgia; Dr. Gerald Grob, Professor of History and Medicine, Rutgers University; Dr. Steven Noll, Professor of History, University of Florida; and Dr. James Trent, Professor of Social Work, Southern Illinois University, for directing me to excellent reference material and for answering more questions than I had a right to ask.

To doctors James Gardiner, neuropsychologist, and Fred Birch, physician and lifelong friend, for willingly giving their time and expertise.

To Mr. Edward Wright, Director, Pinecrest Developmental Center, Pineville, Louisiana, and Mr. Carol McGee, Medical Librarian, Central Louisiana State Hospital, Pineville, Louisiana, for personal tours of their respective institutions.

To Jennie Shortridge, without whose editorial comments and suggestions this would have been a lesser story.

To Neal Coats, Trevor Casper, Stan Kolodzie, George Covington, Phil Reed, and George Penley, for reading portions of the manuscript and sharing honest critiques. To my agent, Jody Rein, for leading the charge and slaying the dragons.

And to my wife, Karen, a first-line editor who pulls no punches, for her unwavering support and enthusiasm for this book.

Della Raye

CHAPTER ONE

The Visitor

Striding through the hospital door with a purpose, she stops quickly at the desk to inquire: "Which room is Madelyn Samuel in, please?"

The nurse recites the number and casually scans the visitor—a vigorous woman of middle age and average height, light wavy hair framing a round, gentle face—attractive but not striking. The eyes, though, the lightest of blue and more than striking, reflect a wisdom born of a life beyond the ordinary.

The visitor smiles warmly and chimes in a delightful Southern voice, "Thank you kindly," turns and walks briskly down the hall.

She notes the patient's closed eyes, pallor, labored breathing, and the thick smell of sickness permeating the room as she steps inside. The frail woman in the bed appears asleep, though it's difficult to tell with the old and infirm. The visitor gently leans over the bed and softly touches a withered hand. Tired old eyes open slowly and begin to focus, then to question. A tender smile lights the strong face looking down on her, but recognition is slow to come.

"It's Della," the visitor says softly. "Della Raye."

The old woman stares deeply into the knowing blue eyes, and the questioning look on her face turns to shock. "Della Raye?" she asks. "Della Raye Rogers?"

"Yes, it's Della Raye," the visitor answers.

Suspicion grips the sick woman's features, then fear. Straining her emaciated body, she pulls back in vain, forcing her white head into the pillow. "My Lord," she marvels, and turns away.

The visitor stands quietly, enduring the strained silence. At length the old woman turns back, studies the face of her guest, and slowly shakes her head. "Della Raye. Why in the world would you come to see me?"

Della Raye pats her arm gently. "Everybody needs a visitor now and then," she says, sliding a chair close beside the bed and seating herself. "How have you been, Miss Samuel? Haven't seen you in a long while."

"I'm not doing so well," Miss Samuel answers, resignation in her voice. "They tell me this might be it. How about you, Della Raye? I heard you got married."

"I did," Della says. "Life's been good to me."

"Children?"

"Yes, I have two sons and five stepdaughters."

"Seven! Big family."

"Yes it is, and I'm proud of all of them."

Being talkative by nature, Della Raye carries the conversation. As she listens to the familiar cadence of Della's voice, the old woman is carried back to another time, another life. Her agitation returns, and she interrupts her guest in midsentence.

"I still can't imagine why you'd come to see me, Della Raye. I mean—the way I was."

"Hush that now," Della Raye says, patting her hand softly. "I don't worry about all that any more, and you needn't either."

Later, as Della Raye prepares to leave, she offers: "I'm sorry to have to run off so soon, but I've got several other visits on my schedule today. I always set Mondays aside for visiting folks. Would you mind if I put you on my list?"

Still eyeing her guest with wonder, the old woman replies. "No, I'd like that a lot. But I don't know if I'll even be here by next Monday."

"You take care of yourself, Miss Samuel," Della Raye says with a parting smile, "and I'll say a prayer for you."

Continuing her busy day, Della Raye drives past the stately halls and neatly-trimmed lawns of the University of Alabama. Down University Street, a mile or so beyond the campus, she passes an ancient metal sign standing between the curb and a long line of trees. The dark sign is unreadable as she drives by, but she knows it by heart. It whispers of a presence hidden behind the trees, an aging mental institution known as Partlow.

Partlow is nearly invisible at first glance. One sees a long line of trees, perhaps the edge of a pleasant grove bordering the sidewalk. But something about the picture is wrong; the line of trees stretches too far. Then in shadows behind the trees, details begin to focus—tall posts with barbed wire strung to their tops: a cruel fence hides there. An arched gate with iron bars comes into view and beyond that, far removed and barely visible through the trees, the buildings materialize. Large and imposing, they dominate the grounds. Suddenly the scene looms, and invades the mind with words such as *mad, insane,* and *asylum.*

Many of the older buildings have been torn down in recent years, and most of the dreadful fence is gone. The old front gate prevails, however, an iron relic lurking in the shadows of drooping trees, its bars a dark reminder of a time when patients were known as inmates. Like the unreadable sign that reveals little or nothing to passersby, Partlow holds secrets of its own. Unlike medical hospitals, whose tall, imposing outlines provide comfort and security to the communities they serve, mental institutions seem to hide behind distance and facades, their very design a mute apology for their existence.

But Della Raye hardly glances at the Partlow sign as she passes. She has souls to visit and hearts to uplift with a smile, a touch, a prayer.

At day's end she returns to her home, a warm and comfortable house on a wooded hillside in the shade of tremendous oaks. Tomorrow is another busy day; at 7:00 A.M. customers will arrive at Della's Beauty Shop, adjacent to her home. She'd rather start before seven o'clock, but her customers refuse to come any earlier.

Della Raye became accustomed to early rising and hard work while growing up in Partlow. When she was a child, all patients capable of manual labor were forced to work long hours every day. The Partlow attendants drove them, and she remembers the attendants well. A few showed compassion for the patients, but most were hard and indifferent. Some, like the dying woman she visited earlier that day, were cruel.

CHAPTER TWO

The Bad Place

Silhouetted in the early morning sun, five people walked down a dusty dirt road in rural Alabama—a reluctant, slow-moving procession. A tall, gangly man in threadbare overalls and dirty felt hat led the way. Three of the four behind him, two women and a small boy, moved with a slow-witted plod. A blond-haired four-year-old girl, the only thing pretty in this picture of poverty, lagged behind. Her blue eyes, alive and alert, shone with intelligence.

One woman moved with a sluggish defiance, her dress ragged, her eyes following the ground like those of a pouting child. "Come on, Dovie, keep up," the gaunt-faced man yelled impatiently. "We gotta catch that train to Birmin'ham."

"Can't move no faster'n I'm goin', Richard," the woman complained.

"I got your chewin' snuff, you know," Richard replied. "And you ain't gettin' none if you don't keep movin'."

"I know," Dovie sighed.

"Ruby, you keep that stupid Dickie Jr. steppin' too," Richard ordered. "He's little, and he ain't got good sense anyhow."

Ruby, thin-faced, stringy-haired, and simple, whined her reply. "He probably don't want to go to that Partlow place no more'n we do."

"Well, that's where you're goin' anyhow. Times is gettin' tougher and tougher, and I can't afford to feed my own, let alone y'all."

The girl, so small for her age she resembled a toddler, spoke up from the rear. "Why do I have to go to Partlow, Uncle Richard? It's a bad place."

"Della Raye, you gotta go with your mama and your aunt and that crazy brother of yours. You're too little not to be with your mama."

"I wanted to go live with them nice people the other day," the tiny girl persisted, "but you ran them off."

"That's enough of your sassy mouth, girl," Richard spat back. "The welfare woman got it fixed up for you to go to Partlow with the rest of this crazy bunch, and that's where you're goin'."

Ruby and Dovie were Richard's sisters; both were, most likely, mentally retarded. Della Raye and Dickie Jr. were Ruby's children. Ruby's older boy, Frank, lived in the county almshouse. All three children were illegitimate, and all were from an unknown father or fathers. Dickie Jr. was two years old, Frank was ten. They, too, were retarded.

Della Raye's only possession was the ragged, filthy dress she wore. It was made from a discarded feed sack. She hardly knew the pleasure of a full stomach; hunger had stalked every day of her short life. She had never tasted ice cream, never petted a puppy, never played with a doll. She seldom smiled.

The year was 1929, and Richard subsisted on the starvation wage of a sharecropper. With the Great Depression looming he could barely support his wife and himself. He had arranged to have all but Dickie Jr. committed to Partlow, a state mental institution in Tuscaloosa.

Although Della Raye was not yet five, the minimum age for admission to Partlow, her uncle had falsely claimed her to be seven. In the bizarre mixture of misfits whom Richard lead down the road to incarceration, the bright-eyed little girl seemed strangely out of place.

Before going to Partlow, Della Raye and her indigent family lived crowded together with Richard and his wife in a run-down sharecropper's shack. Prior to that, they stayed in the county almshouse, a filthy pit described by a social worker as a "dreadful place for a child."

My uncle just rounded us up. We were starving, and I guess he didn't know what else to do with us. We had no food, no clothes, no place to stay. The records say we were in the poorhouse at one time, but I can't recall it. I don't remember much about life before Partlow; I remember playing some with Frank, eating apples, things like that. I don't remember ever really feeling happy when I was little. I loved my mama, but I don't think she cared much for me.

A few days before we went to Partlow, a young couple came to Uncle Richard's house wanting to adopt me. Uncle Richard was out working in the field at the time. I don't remember it all, but Mama told me about it later. The couple just had one child, a little boy, and couldn't have any more. They made a good living and told Mama they would raise me as their own and see that I got a good education. I liked them, and Mama was going to let them take me.

Uncle Richard's wife was telling Mama to hurry, because if he came back, he wasn't going to like what she was doing. Mama was about to sign her "X" on the papers when Uncle Richard came through the door. He saw what was going on and got mad and started cussing and hollering at the people and telling them to get out.

We didn't know we were going to Partlow then, but the young couple did. I guess the welfare lady had told them. "Why can't we take her?" they asked Uncle Richard. "You're just going to send her to that Partlow place and lock her up."

Uncle Richard wouldn't hear of it, told them I had to go with my mama. Then he ran them off. I felt hard toward him about that for a long time.

They walked through miles of wooded hills, which were practically devoid of houses, to reach the train station in Athens, Alabama. Exhausted, Ruby carried Dickie Jr. in her arms as they trudged into town. As they neared the station, several men suddenly stepped out of the crowd, lined up beside Richard, and turned to face Ruby. Richard stepped forward, held out his arms, and said, "Give me Dickie Jr., Ruby. He ain't old enough to go to Partlow."

For a moment it didn't register, then a surprised horror gripped Ruby's simple face. She jerked back violently. "No! No! You can't take him!" she screamed. "He's mine. He's my baby!" She whirled and started to run.

Richard leaped forward and grabbed Ruby from behind. The other men grabbed Dickie Jr. and tried to wrestle him out of her arms. She held to her boy tightly, screaming and fighting viciously; but they ripped the squalling child from her, turned, and dashed into the crowd.

As Dickie's screams faded into the distance, Ruby stopped struggling, dropped her head, and sobbed in pitiful defeat. "You're the devil, Richard. There ain't nothin' you won't do." Richard didn't answer. He released his grip on Ruby's waist and herded them onto a train bound for Birmingham. Grim-faced and sullen, he rode with them.

Della Raye had never ridden in a train nor seen one, but the novelty of the experience escaped her. Dickie Jr.'s screams had terrified her, along with thoughts of the place they were going—Partlow. The couple, who had come to adopt her, had said it was a place where they locked you up, a bad place. Della leaned on her mama, crying as the train bore them along, but Ruby stared out the window and offered little solace. As they steamed through the northern Alabama countryside of wooded hills, fields, and bright meadows, all she could see was Richard's silent face; all she could feel was fear.

They got off the train in Birmingham and boarded a bus for Tuscaloosa. A bus ride was a new experience as well, but still she hardly noticed. She only knew it was bringing them closer to Partlow.

Della Raye had stopped crying by the time they reached the city, and as the bustle on the streets caught her attention, she stood up in the seat to look. Then the bus rounded a corner and the brakes began to squeal. She turned to Ruby and broke into tears again. They turned into a line of trees that concealed a narrow dirt drive, and a barred gate loomed before them. Della's face twisted in terror as her crying became a frightened wail, but her mama paid no attention.

Stern-faced attendants stood waiting at the gate, all dressed in white uniforms. They stepped onto the bus with a cold, businesslike air and began to direct her family and others out the door. Crying hysterically and gasping for breath, Della Raye ran to the back. "No! Stay away from me!" she screamed at the pursuing attendants.

Richard watched silently as strong hands grabbed his niece, shoved her off the bus and through the iron gate.

As the bus pulled away a stern voice ordered, "Grownups in one line, kids in the other." Della Raye fought the attendants, trying mightily to cling to Ruby, but they propelled her into a line with the other children and shoved her along. In the melee of separation, manhandling, and marching to somewhere unknown, she lost track of her mama. When they slowed and stopped at the entrance to a large building, Della looked to the side, saw the other line several yards away, and spotted Ruby.

"Mama!" she cried, and broke out of an attendant's grip. She ran to the other line and grabbed her mama around the legs.

The startled attendant pointed a finger and shouted to a supervisor, "Look there, Miss Hennessy. That little girl's broke loose and run over to the other line!"

The supervisor glanced at Della Raye, waved her hand, and scoffed. "Aw, let her be," she said. "She hasn't got good sense anyhow."

On gently-rolling hills amidst great spreading oaks and tall Southern pines, two patient dormitories rose, stark and authoritative. Long and rectangular, the brick behemoths dominated the grounds. One stood three stories high, the other two. A trio of single-story buildings hunkered among the giants: the kitchen and main dining room, the laundry and central heating plant, and a disquieting structure known as the Untidy Building.

Della Raye would live in the Main Building, a two-story dorm with tall columns commanding an entrance that opened into a rotunda in the center. Long wings extended left and right from the rotunda, a heavy locked door guarding the entrance to each. A staircase on either side led to the second-floor wings and more locked doors. Each wing formed a single long room on each floor—a ward filled with mental patients of one kind or another.

Patients, or inmates as they were known in official records, were strictly separated by gender, and ate separately as well. Male and female patients were never allowed to intermingle; they could neither touch nor talk to one another at any time.

All attendants in the male wards were men and all in the female wards were women. Each carried a large ring of keys and continually unlocked and locked doors behind them as they moved between buildings and wards.

Differing mentality levels further separated the patients. According to official nomenclature of the day, the retarded, or feebleminded, fell into three categories according to mental capacity: moron, imbecile, and idiot. Morons ranked highest in intelligence or closest to "normal"; imbeciles ranked mid-range; and idiots were the lowest. (Those familiar terms, long since drowned in tasteless jokes and derisive slang, have lost virtually all technical merit.)

Morons and imbeciles were known as "high grades." Most high grades were ambulatory and with proper instruction could learn to feed and dress themselves. Some could attend to personal hygiene as well, though many needed help in that area. High grades were housed in large barracks-style wards separate from the low grades.

The low-level idiots, many of whom were unaware of their own existence, presented a greater problem. Some idiots spent their days strapped in wheelchairs or fouled beds, while others shuffled about the room jabbering and shaking their heads continually. Still others sat on benches and drooled, babbled, or simply stared, tongues lolling sickly from their rolling heads. Horribly bent limbs, deformed craniums, and twisted faces were commonplace. Distorted spines and wrenched rib cages skewed their postures into hideous contortions. Constant tremors lashed their knotted bodies or jerked and shook their twisted limbs. Many breathed laboriously and loud, and could not talk. Shrieks, screams, and primal cries filled the air day and night. All this in a horrid space named by some master of understatement—a stinking, howling hell known as the Untidy Ward.

If Richard truly believed that Della Raye belonged with her mother, he might have inquired into the living conditions at Partlow before having them committed. Adults and children lived on separate wards. It made no difference if they were mother and daughter; she lost her mama the moment they entered the gate. It seemed to matter little to Ruby at the time, but Della Raye was bright, and she was four.

Della Raye became a wild animal that day. As flustered attendants herded their new charge to the high-grade ward, she howled, screamed, and fought them all the way. When they finally arrived, an attendant inserted a key into the lock, twisted it, and swung open the heavy door.

She stopped screaming. Flanked by attendants to block her escape, Della Raye stared down the bunker-like corridor: a long, colorless room with high ceilings, drab and hopelessly crowded, a sea of narrow beds butted barracks-style against each wall. Twenty-two cots on either side framed a narrow aisle down the middle—forty-four patients in a single room.

But the room didn't concern Della Raye. The patients did. A bizarre crowd of strangers turned to stare. Standing in the middle aisle and the spaces between the beds, they stopped their nervous milling and stared as one. Though some appeared as normal as she, others were marked by strange postures—heads and shoulders drooping forward, arms dangling, mouths agape, and staring vacantly. Some jerked and shook with uncontrollable tremors while others sat limply on their beds, slumped and slack-jawed, gazing with empty eyes.

Della Raye was the smallest there. Her body shaking with fear, she stared into the ward—a tiny person at the door to purgatory. She shrank back against the legs of the attendants and reached up for help, but none was there. They stood rigid, offering neither comfort nor protection. Della Raye scanned the forbidding crowd another long moment, then ripped the silence with a scream. She charged headlong into the older girls. Pushing, shoving, and bouncing off legs, she leaped ahead of the startled attendants.

Della Raye ran, cried, and screamed the entire day. By evening her tear-stained cheeks were bright red and her hair and clothes an angry mess, but she was relentless. No amount of talking, pleading, or cajoling would reach her, and they could not make her go to bed. Forty-three patients lay awake as she careened from one end of the ward to the other screaming, "Mama! Mama!" beating her fists on the locked doors and driving the harried attendants wild.

They grabbed her, spanked her, and slapped her hard in the face, but the roughness only made it worse. Della Raye backed against a wall between two beds screaming, "I hate you! I hate you!" and kicked, scratched, and bit anyone who dared come near.

It was a long night for everyone.

Della Raye finally stopped crying and fell asleep from exhaustion. When she awoke the next morning she cried no more. The attendants bathed her, washed her hair, and fitted her with a plain cotton dress and clunky institutional shoes. She remained reasonably cooperative through it all, though watchful and wary, and she would not talk. Everyone kept a close eye on her, the previous night having gained her instant notoriety throughout the asylum.

The crowded ward felt stifling, engulfing. The stale stench of human bodies permeated the air. Not a single picture adorned the walls; even the simplest stools and chairs were scarce. The forty-four metal cots scarcely had leg room between them, and a barrier of heavy wire mesh hung behind each curtainless window, the same wire that enclosed the second- and third-floor balconies, making cages of them.

Della Raye had no belongings other than the little dress, underpants and shoes she had just acquired. When an attendant pointed out that she now had her own locker, she was unimpressed. In the days following they showed her the basics of institutional life. She paid close attention, or as close as a little girl can, but she hardly reacted to any of it.

Partlow operated on a strict daily routine, and patients had many rules to follow. Della Raye may have been quiet and watchful, but she didn't accept rules at face value, nor was she an altogether compliant child. Whenever she disagreed with the attendants about anything, she stoically defied them.

They all agreed the new little girl was a tough case, especially frustrating in the face of discipline. Neither spanking nor slapping would dent her determination, and the first time an angry attendant grabbed a handful of hair and yanked it, Della Raye stood and stared at her with sullen defiance.

The amazing stubbornness had them all shaking their heads. One quality was unbelievable in a child her age. Regardless of the punishment or how rough they applied it, Della Raye would not cry.

Her unbending defiance would chart the course of Della Raye's life in Partlow. It became her curse, and ultimately her salvation.

Partlow opened in 1923 as the Alabama Home for Mental Defectives. Four years later its name was changed to the Partlow State School for Mental Deficients to honor its founder, Dr. W. D. Partlow. Dr. Partlow gained national fame as a leader in the field of mental health at an early age, and served as the head of all mental facilities in Alabama from 1919 to 1949. As the director's fame grew, his namesake asylum became known simply as Partlow.

Beginning with a single dormitory designed to accommodate one hundred and sixty patients, Partlow grew more rapidly than its founder could have imagined. Only a few weeks after it opened, the dormitory filled to capacity. Another one-story building was added the following year, but that didn't solve the problem for long. By 1930 Partlow had nearly four hundred patients and applications on file for many more.

Adding the word school to Partlow's name may have represented an early hope for the institution, but the Great Depression foreclosed any possibility of providing educational opportunities. The nation was undergoing economic chaos and, especially in the Deep South, extreme poverty. A lack of state funding, along with an ever-increasing patient population, destroyed any hope for meaningful treatment. Patient care degenerated into little more than human warehousing.

Not only was Partlow overcrowded and poorly funded, but also terribly understaffed. And though employment of any sort was difficult to find during the Depression, the attendant's job was one of the worst. Attendants worked long hours, were not allowed to marry, and practically lived with the patients. They ate their meals in the main dining room and slept crowded several to a room in small apartments on the top floors of the dormitories. They could leave the grounds only at designated times, and a strict curfew regulated their return. An attendant's workday consisted of twelve to fourteen hours on the feet. With room and board considered the lion's share of their pay, their state salary amounted to something like twenty to thirty dollars a month.

In 1929 the state appropriation for all supervisor's and nurse's salaries totaled $20,300. Such conditions could hardly attract a premium work force. Most attendants came from poor backgrounds and had little or no education. They received no training at Partlow either, and worked most of the time without supervision.

W. D. Partlow directed the state facilities from his office in Bryce Hospital, an older, larger mental institution in Tuscaloosa. His Assistant Superintendent, Dr. L. H. Woodruff, ran Partlow on a day-to-day basis.

Dr. Woodruff was the only physician on staff when Della Raye arrived in 1929. He and a handful of supervisors ran the institution. The supervisors roamed in and out of the wards intermittently. Under the crowded conditions, neither they nor Dr. Woodruff had time to oversee the attendants nor to control the way they treated patients.

All female attendants dressed alike: white nurse's bonnets, small white aprons, white uniforms with narrow blue stripes. Supervisors wore the same bonnets and aprons, but uniforms of solid white instead of stripes.

All patients, adults and children alike, were known as boys and girls. Patients were addressed by their first names, but in official records they were called boys and girls regardless of age, an uncomplimentary reference to their inferior mental capacity. Employees generally maintained a certain aloofness with patients and were not allowed to express affection or show favoritism. Patients addressed them as "Miss" along with their surname, though some became known as Mama. To call an employee by her given name was strictly forbidden.

"All right, girls," a horsy woman's voice boomed through the ward. "It's time to get in them beds. You better go the toilet now if you need to, 'cause I'm fixin' to lock the door to that bathroom in a minute."

"Della Raye, you better get up off your little rear and go use the bathroom. After I lock the door you ain't gonna get in there."

"But I don't have to go now, Mama Herman," Della said.

"Well, you're gonna wish you had pretty soon," the attendant replied.

The light switches operated with a key, so only the attendants could control them. At bedtime the attendants turned out the lights in the wards and bathrooms, and to prevent the girls from getting out of bed continually to use the toilet, they locked the bathroom doors. The doors normally stayed locked for two hours, then an attendant or supervisor came through and unlocked them. Afterwards, the bathroom remained open the rest of the night, but was left dark to conserve electricity.

This bathroom door-locking made it difficult for some of the girls, especially the little ones. As children are prone to do, they sometimes put off using the bathroom before bedtime; then a short while after lights out they would have to go. Having no other choice, if a girl couldn't wait until the door was unlocked, she had to wet her bed and sleep in it the rest of the night.

A few minutes after the lights went out and the attendant left, Della Raye had to go. "Hey," she whispered to the girl in the next bed. "I gotta pee."

"The door's locked," her neighbor answered.

"I know it, but I gotta pee, bad!"

"Then you'll have to do it in the bed like everybody else does," came the unwelcome reply.

Della Raye lay in the dark, needing to go badly but unwilling to soil the bed she had to sleep in. She slowly sat up, reached down to the foot of her bed, and pulled the sheet free. Taking the lower end of the sheet in both hands, she wadded it into a tight ball and urinated into it. Then she hung the end of the sheet over the foot of the bed to dry, covered herself, and went to sleep.

It smelled bad until it dried out, but the ward smelled like urine and a lot of other things most of the time anyway, so nobody ever noticed.

Old-fashioned radiators heated the ward—the steamy, hissing kind that stood upright against the wall. The near-boiling water that circulated through their metal pipes kept their sides extremely hot. And though the radiators didn't heat the ward well, standing next to one on a cold day made a patient feel cozy and warm.

One chilly morning Della Raye and an older girl crowded close to one of the radiators. Holding their hands near the hot pipes and rubbing them together, they grinned at each other and enjoyed the warmth. Suddenly the girl began to sway on her feet. Looking up into her face with alarm, Della saw her eyes roll back in their sockets; her head and body begin to shake violently. Wheezing loudly and frothing at the mouth, the girl stiffened and shook in jerking spasms. Her legs crumbled under her and she fell forward.

Della Raye stood in speechless horror as the girl's face and neck slid down the singeing sides of the radiator. Finally she found her voice and screamed, "Mama Leonard!"

A large woman charged past her, shoving patients out of the way as she ran, and pulled the convulsing girl off the radiator. Badly burned, though unaware of it, the girl chomped her jaws together and clacked her teeth loudly. Mama Leonard jerked her head back and forced something into her mouth; Della Raye thought it looked like a spoon.

Other attendants came rushing to help as the burned girl writhed on the floor, bubbly hisses escaping her clenched teeth. Della stood back among the other dazed patients and watched wide-eyed as the women applied towels and rags to the girl's burns and fought to control her wildly convulsing body.

The girl slowly stopped shaking and her breathing returned to normal. Finally she lay quietly on the floor, her eyes closed as if in sleep. Holding the towels against her burns, the attendants lifted her onto a stretcher and carried her away.

Mama Leonard—a plain, heavyset woman with short, kinky hair square-cut across the back—was a stout, matronly figure and a favorite among the girls, especially the little ones. She didn't openly display affection, but she treated them with kindness and compassion.

Still shaking from the grisly accident she had just witnessed, Della Raye didn't notice Mama Leonard until she kneeled down and looked into her frightened eyes. "I know it scared you, Della," the big woman said kindly. "It's too bad she got burned, but she just has them fits ever now and then. Some of the others in here do too. You'll see them do the same thing one of these days. When it happens, just holler for me like you did."

"Why'd you put that thing in her mouth?" Della asked.

"So she wouldn't bite her tongue off, honey," Mama Leonard said.

In her short life Della Raye had never heard of epilepsy, nor did she realize that epileptics were commonly committed to mental institutions. Medication was not yet available to control their symptoms, and even if an epileptic appeared otherwise normal, doctors considered the seizures an indication of feeblemindedness. One of several ways an intelligent person could end up in Partlow.

Della remained determined not to shed tears in front of the attendants, but later that night the scene of the girl falling against the radiator returned to haunt her. She lay in the darkness and cried alone. She could hear other girls in the ward crying too. No one came to comfort them.

The building that contained the kitchen and main dining room stood in the center of the grounds. Because low-level patients could not leave the Untidy Wards, their food was carried to them, while the high-grade girls ate in the dining room.

Every day at exactly the same time, the girls would form two lines, each holding the hand of the one next to her. Again at the very same minute each day, an attendant would unlock the door and march them, holding hands two-by-two, to the dining room. They would all stop outside and wait while the attendant unlocked the door, then proceed inside.

A huge, hollow room, stark and impersonal, its white walls long since faded to gray, the dining room exuded the noxious smell of cleanser rather than food. Slick floors sloped from all sides into a central drain that wreaked of old meals better forgotten.

As the banging of pots, pans and silverware echoed from the recesses of the kitchen, located to the rear, each girl walked to an assigned table and found her assigned seat. Two long benches flanked each one, seating four girls to a side. A stool at either end seated two more for a total of ten per table. When the dining room door had been locked behind them and every girl was standing at her seat, together they chanted the doxology: "Praise God from whom all blessings flow. Praise Him all creatures here below."

A visiting minister was once nearly moved to tears at the spectacle. After watching a group of retarded children stumble into the dining room, find their seats with difficulty, and struggle through the doxology, he shook his head and muttered, "And they can still sing His praises."

When the prayer was finished, the girls sat down and waited quietly to be served. Talking in the dining room was forbidden.

A staff of patients provided free labor for the kitchen. Under the stern supervision of Partlow employees, they prepared, cooked, and served the food. Each girl sat with her hands in her lap while the kitchen patients dished out the meal, then on command the girls would pick up their silverware and begin eating the institutional fare—watery, starchy, and bland.

Most of the male patients lived and worked several miles from Partlow on a state-owned farm called the Boys Colony ("boys" meaning adults as well as children). The few male patients who did live at Partlow proper never ate in the dining room with the girls; though for some reason a few male attendants sat off in one corner while the girls ate, perhaps as a show of force to help keep order.

Also to keep order and to enforce the no-talking rule, several attendants and kitchen employees stood watch over the girls as they ate. They hovered around the perimeter of the dining room like sentinel hawks, and if one of them saw a girl talking she wrote down her name. Later in the week the names were compiled, and anyone who appeared on the list was "posted." Posted patients lost the privilege of watching the weekly movie on Thursday night.

I had a hard time with that. I tried so hard to be good, but I guess I talked too much. It seemed like I was always getting posted.

Della Raye came to know many faces in the kitchen, particularly Partlow employees with reputations. A thin, masculine tyrant named Betty Myers ran the kitchen. A vile, tiger of a woman—wiry, foul-mouthed and severe—Miss Myers was known for cruelty to patients who worked under her.

A big, dumpy woman named Myra Helpman also loved to flaunt her authority around the kitchen. She, too, was cruel to patients, and even was known to take personal belongings from them.

Another pathetic employee posed no threat to anyone. At dinner one day, several girls were seen looking around toward one side of the dining room and giggling under their breath. The girl next to Della Raye elbowed her in the ribs and pointed at the wall. Mona McCurty, a fat, sloppy, kitchen employee, had the watch duty. She was not standing like the others, though, nor was she even watching the girls. She sat slumped in a chair, frazzled hair poking out all over her head and ragged denim pants extending from beneath her dress. Mona sat talking to herself in a constant murmur, shaking her head, twisting her face into outlandish contortions, and wrinkling up her nose first one way and then the other, all the while twiddling her thumbs and watching them with rapt fascination.

They all knew that Mona was an employee. Soon every girl in the dining room, the badly-retarded, simple, and bright, was looking at the woman and fighting to suppress a giggle as the other attendants tried to shush them and motioned them to stop staring.

Wasn't that ugly of us, making fun of her? She was worse than some of the patients. She should have been a patient herself.

The kitchen attendants were not the only employees who could be cruel. Mama Herman, a huge, solid, cotton bale of a woman, was notorious.

She was big, and tall. She must have weighed three hundred and fifty, maybe four hundred pounds, and she was a bully.

Middle-aged with a square, pig face and physically power- ful, Mama Herman was feared by every patient in Partlow. She reveled in that distinction, and her actions kept her reputa- tion intact. Besides physical abuse, locking patients out of the bathrooms was Mama Herman's favorite trick. She did it at odd times to catch them by surprise.

An employee like Mama Herman could freely inflict pain and misery on patients with no fear of retribution whatsoever. If a more compassionate attendant witnessed another one bullying or mistreating a patient, nothing was said. An unwritten law stated that no employee would interfere with another's methods nor report them to a supervisor. They lived by that law, and controlled the institution by it.

Two young supervisors oversaw the female wards: Millie Hennessy and Madelyn Samuel.

Millie Hennessy held the position of Senior Supervisor at Partlow for all the years that Della was there. Hard-working, loyal, and conscientious, Miss Hennessy had drawn a sad hand in the game of life. Short, dumpy, and bowlegged to the point of deformity, she walked her rounds with a rocking, exaggerated limp. The lame woman kept herself neat and clean, but wire-rimmed glasses and a head of shortly-cropped black hair did nothing to improve a face painfully plain.

Miss Hennessy lived alone in a room within a small frame building known as the Schoolhouse. She took her job seriously and could be stern and tough when necessary, but beneath the crippled, deformed exterior, God had given Millie Hennessy a heart. If she caught one of the girls doing something against the rules, such as sewing a piece of clothing for herself, Miss Hennessy would stop and chat with her and ignore the act completely.

Madelyn Samuel had everything in life that Millie Hennessy did not. She stood trim, stately, and poised; her light, bouncy hair, naturally wavy and nearly blond, framed a beautiful face. Miss Samuel was married, one of the few employees allowed the privilege. She and her husband, a supervisor in the male wards, had met and secretly married while working at Bryce. Their marriage had been discovered, but both were highly valued employees whom the director didn't want to lose. Instead of being fired, they were transferred to Partlow as supervisors and provided a cottage on the grounds in which to live.

Miss Samuel kept order in the wards and saw that everything operated smoothly, but for all her good looks and good fortune, she didn't appreciate life as Millie Hennessy did. She seldom smiled and showed little respect for anyone, certainly not the patients. She lived to strut in and out of the wards shouting orders and flaunting her authority, unless she happened to be quietly stalking a patient to catch her in some petty unauthorized act. Madelyn Samuel would never have children. Her only joy in life was lording her authority over the less fortunate, her only legacy a haunting memory of the same.

In order to operate a sprawling institution with minimal funding and a skeleton staff, Partlow required all patients, teenage and older, to work full time—all those who could work, that is. Since most of the idiots and many of the lower-level imbeciles were incapable of performing even the simplest tasks, high-grade inmates made premium stock. Their free labor enabled the institution to become self-sustaining.

The Boys Colony, where most of the male patients lived and worked, raised crops and livestock to feed the inmates of Partlow. A large-scale farming operation covering nearly two thousand acres, the Colony provided beef, pork, chicken and vegetables for patient consumption and transported eggs and milk to the main kitchen daily. Of course, high-grade patients made the most desirable farm workers for the Colony.

Partlow had its own clothing and linen factory as well, the sewing room—a cavernous space filled with foot-operated sewing machines where female patients worked long hours making sheets, pillowcases, and every item of clothing worn by patients. Even the stockings, bras, and panties the girls wore came from the sewing room.

Growing up in Partlow was like joining the army as a child, a regimentation that would become as much a part of Della Raye as eating and breathing. Every minute of the day, every phase of a patient's life, was orchestrated according to strict routine. Every morning at 6:00, a loud whistle sounded across the grounds to rouse the patients. The girls jumped up quickly, as each had to dress, make her own bed, and line up for breakfast.

Unlike the older girls, the smaller ones didn't work full time; however, even they had regular jobs. Every morning when they returned from breakfast, Della Raye and several other little girls had to clean the bathroom.

The patient bathroom was a dank hollow cave that offered no privacy. Amid smelly drains that clogged too often and leaky pipes covered with rust, an exposed line of toilets crouched side by side with no partitions to separate them. Half a dozen shower heads protruded from the opposite wall, facing the stark line of stools like probing eyes.

Della Raye's main task was to empty the water from the five toilet stools and scrub them out. First she dipped out most of the water with a can, then soaked the rest into a large towel and wrung it into a drain. When all the stools were dry, she and the other girls scrubbed the insides of them by hand as well as the sinks and the claw foot bathtub used by crippled patients. The attendants watched and checked their work.

In another labor-saving measure, adult patients were placed in charge of the younger ones. And like the attendants, the patients could use whatever punishment they chose to control their charges with no fear of repercussion. If an adult patient slapped a child or knocked her to the ground, no attendant ever witnessed the act. The watchdog patients who were put in charge of others tended to be fiercely loyal to the attendants who appointed them, and they could be meaner to their fellow patients than even the employees. What better way to garner an attendant's favor than to do her dirty work for her?

Each building had its own yard, an area where the smaller children played. When they finished their cleaning chores, at exactly 9:00 A.M., the younger girls lined up to go to the yard. In the yard they jumped rope, played hopscotch and other such games under the watchful eyes of attendants and older patients. Della Raye continued to rebel at the rules and to react with defiance when punished, but she got along reasonably well with the other girls, and she loved to play in the yard. Occasionally their play was interrupted; a kitchen employee would come to the yard and take some of the younger girls to the kitchen to shell peas, clean beans, and other such mundane tasks.

I hated that. I'd try to hide when I saw one of them coming, but they'd find me and make me go over there anyway.

One day she refused. "No, I want to stay here and play," Della told the patient in charge. "I don't want to go to no stinking kitchen and shell peas all day."

The simple woman shook a menacing finger in her face. "Girl, they want you to go to work," she said loudly. "Now you get goin' to the kitchen like I said."

"No!" Della said, stomping her feet. "I'm not going to no kitchen!" At that the patient grabbed Della, slapped her across the face, and ordered her once more to go to the kitchen.

Della jerked loose from her grip. "No," she said. Her face reddening from the hard slap, she stood and looked up defiantly into the woman's eyes.

An attendant who had been watching the confrontation walked over and told the patient, "You go see to the others. I'll take care of her."

The attendant grabbed Della by the collar and jerked her roughly toward the building. As soon as they entered the ward the woman grabbed her by the hair with one hand and began slapping her cheeks with the other.

"Who the hell you think you are, little girl?!" the attendant yelled. Back and forth she whacked her cheeks, first with the palm of her hand then with the back. The force of the blows rocked Della's head and threatened to rip out her hair, but she didn't make a sound.

"What's wrong with you?!" the woman screamed. She flipped Della over and beat her on the back and bottom until her own hand hurt. When the livid attendant finally released her, Della walked to her bed, turned, and sat down. Her quivering face was swelled bright red, a trickle of blood ran from her nose. With eyes water-filled but stony, Della Raye clamped her jaw and glared at the woman with silent rage.

"What's wrong with you?!" the attendant screamed again. "You ain't right, girl! You ain't right!" She turned and stomped toward the door, then stopped, whirled, and pointed a threatening finger at Della Raye.

"Damn you, girl. We'll get you. One way or the other, we'll make you cry."

CHAPTER THREE

Yea Though I Walk

Viktor Frankl, an Austrian psychiatrist who endured years of horror in Nazi death camps, wrote of his experience in his book, *Man's Search For Meaning*. While many prisoners simply gave up and died, Frankl noted, a few managed not only to survive the ghastly conditions but also to rise above their circumstance and preserve a modicum of human dignity.

Frankl lost his wife, his mother, his father, and a brother to Hitler's ovens, but through strong personal beliefs and a good deal of luck, he survived the ordeal. One of the most astonishing qualities he noted among survivors was a strong sense of humor. Amidst a life filled with unspeakable horror and devoid of hope, some actually found bits of humor and used them to momentarily lift their spirits. Frankl described humor as "another of the soul's weapons in the fight for self-preservation. It is well known that humor, more than anything else in the human makeup, can afford an aloofness and an ability to rise above any situation, even if only for a few seconds."

Della Raye is one of Frankl's survivors. From her youngest years, she demonstrated an irrepressible sense of humor, a gift that served her well in Partlow.

Partlow had no minister on staff, nor was it affiliated with any religious organization. Various church groups came to the asylum on Sundays, however, and performed on the stage in the Schoolhouse. Both girls and boys (adults and children) could attend, though each sex sat on opposite sides of the room.

Because the church groups were discouraged from preaching to the patients or reading the Bible, their programs consisted mostly of funny stories and gospel singing. One determined minister, however, insisted on teaching biblical lessons. Preacher Paulsen, a wizened little man with a bald head, picked up the Bible on his first visit, and squinting through his narrow reading glasses, began to read. Before he could finish more than a few lines, Miss Hennessy stood up and interrupted him.

"All right, that's all for today," the supervisor said loudly, and motioned for the patients to leave. When all the patients were gone, Miss Hennessy told the obviously shaken minister, "They don't understand that kind of stuff—stories from the Bible, Jesus, anything like that. They need to be entertained sometimes, but we don't want anybody preaching to them."

Preacher Paulsen disagreed. He couldn't understand why the patients (who, after all, were the same as other people), shouldn't be told of the hope the Bible promised to all of God's children. The preacher was a prudent man, nevertheless, and refrained from voicing his dissension to the supervisor.

"If you come here again, don't be preaching on the Bible," Miss Hennessy told the man. "We forbid it." He nodded and left.

The next time Preacher Paulsen came, Miss Hennessy listened closely. He didn't read directly from the Bible, but in his talk he began a line of reasoning that sounded suspiciously biblical to her. "You don't throw away your old shoes when you get new shoes," the preacher told his attentive audience, "and you don't discard your old friends when you get new ones. You don't forget your old beliefs when you learn new things either, and you never discard hope."

Miss Hennessy exploded. Jumping to her feet as fast as her crippled legs could move, she shouted, "I told you there'd be none of that!" and stormed for the preacher in a limping charge.

Startled at the violent reaction, Preacher Paulsen tried to explain. "I wasn't . . . " he managed, but the supervisor nearly ran him over.

"Get outta here!" she hollered into his terror-stricken face. "I told you we wouldn't have any more of that!"

The preacher reeled backward and nearly lost his balance. With Miss Hennessy yelling insanely, the little man turned, ran from the building, and shot into his car. Hastily starting the engine, he jammed the car into gear, plunged forward, and crashed into an electrical pole. Without stopping to assess the damage, Preacher Paulsen backed away from the pole in a whirl of gravel and dust, turned, and raced from the grounds.

Della Raye had never been exposed to any form of religion, but she found the singing programs entertaining. She and her girlfriend Maryanne, being the two smallest there, always sat in front. One minister decided to teach his listeners to sing—an ambitious undertaking considering that his audience consisted largely of feebleminded people. All were enthusiastic about the singing lessons, however, and more than willing to follow the minister's lead.

With a smile on his face and hope in his heart, the naive minister began. "Listen to me first, then after I sing a line I'll point to you all and you sing it just like I did." His choir-to-be responded eagerly. Huge grins, exaggerated nods, wildly waving arms, rocking bodies, squeals, grunts, and a litany of unintelligible sounds told him they were ready.

"I love you truly, truuly, truuuly," the minister sang slowly, then pointed to his gleefully awaiting audience. When the patients began to sing—a unique response a bit less than melodious—Della covered her mouth but began giggling loudly. Maryanne looked at her in horror, as did the beleaguered choir director who had enough on his hands without further distraction. Miss Hennessy, standing stiffly on the sidelines, shook a stern finger at Della Raye and frowned.

When the patients finished their line, they all leaned forward, grinned proudly, and looked at their director with taut anticipation. Della Raye sat still, her hands forced stiffly into her lap, her lips clenched tightly. The determined minister managed a tentative smile and repeated, "I love you truly, truuly, truuuly," and again gave the cue to his eager choir.

Della couldn't handle it. As one of the strangest attempts at harmony in the history of music filled the room, her laughter did too. When finally the singing was finished, Della's giggling under control, and Miss Hennessy's brow deeply furrowed, the exasperated minister praised his impromptu choir, and to their deep disappointment, called an end to his first and only singing lesson.

Another church group came once a month. As always, Della Raye and Maryanne listened from the middle seats in the front row. For some pieces the entire group sang together; for others they separated into duos, trios, and quartets. One tall, middle-aged lady loved to perform alone. The first time she sang solo, she stood at the center of the stage, directly in front of Della Raye and Maryanne. The girls looked up and gave the lady their strict attention. She began singing softly, but her voice quickly gained strength and the volume climbed higher and higher. Within a minute the room was filled with high, falsetto tones that threatened to vibrate the woman's vocal chords apart.

Della Raye did come apart. Grabbing her mouth with both hands, she rocked back and forth and giggled insanely while the nervous lady fought to finish her piece. When she was done she cast a terribly uncomfortable glance at Della. Miss Hennessy looked at the ceiling and shook her head.

When the group had gone, Miss Hennessy took her aside. "Now listen, Della Raye," the head supervisor said. "Those church people come here to sing for us and try to entertain us. It's not nice to be laughing at them."

Della nodded her little head sincerely. "Okay, Miss Hennessy. I'll try to do better."

A month later the church group returned. Both supervisors, Miss Samuel and Miss Hennessy, were standing at the back of the room. Before Della sat down, Miss Hennessy reminded her, "Now Della Raye, you remember what I told you about laughing." Della nodded earnestly and walked to the front with Maryanne.

The church people filed onto the stage, greeted their audience warmly, and began to sing. Loud cheers, exaggerated clapping, guttural grunts, and assorted murmurs indicated everyone was enjoying the show. Della Raye and Maryanne paid close attention and listened quietly.

Well into the program, the tall lady stepped forward, smiled grandly, bowed, and prepared to sing. Della Raye was determined to be good. As the solo began, she sat primly with her hands in her lap and her chin forced tightly against her chest. Low and soothing at first, the woman's voice slowly began to rise, and rise, and rise. Soon resembling more of a controlled scream than song, her tortured tones reverberated off the walls and ceiling as the skin covering her throat vibrated like the head of a drum. Della Raye grew wide-eyed, grabbed her mouth, and held it tightly. The lady held the note, and Della held her mouth.

She might have made it—if Maryanne hadn't elbowed her in the ribs. One of Della's hands slipped slightly, and a gasp of air escaped her tightly-pursed lips. She caught herself, though, and held on, until Maryanne poked her in the ribs again and began giggling herself. Della Raye released a loud, sputtering wheeze, which blew her hands from her mouth, then she rocked forward in a wild spate of giggling and laughing. The church lady looked at her in alarm. The great volume that filled the room faded rapidly as Miss Hennessy and Miss Samuel quickstepped for the front. The two of them picked Della Raye up and carried her to the back and out the door, giggling uncontrollably all the way. As the confused audience turned and watched them carry Della Raye out, the embarrassed singer retreated to her seat on the stage.

I've often wondered what that poor woman thought about a little child in a mental institution making fun of her singing.

With the aid of a caring attendant, the high-grade girls at Partlow formed singing groups of their own. Being a popular performer in patient activities, Della Raye sang in a quartet. On Sundays when no church groups came to entertain them, the girls improvised their own programs.

Dr. Woodruff was a lover of gospel music and often attended Partlow's singing programs. Short and stout with a head of dark, wavy hair, his square face accentuated by thick-rimmed glasses, the assistant director exuded a smug, confident air, an attitude easily maintained in a world where hundreds of uneducated people lived under his control, most of whom were feebleminded. Dr. Woodruff always sat in front at the singings, where he would flash a patronizing smile, request his favorite hymn, "In the Garden," and join in the singing.

Lorita Fricard (Low-reeta), a flamboyant patient known to everyone, lived to participate in programs. It didn't matter what kind of program—anything that gave her an opportunity to draw attention to herself worked for Lorita. Although Lorita was blue-eyed with prematurely white hair and a reasonably pretty face, the rest of her masked any possible appearance of normalcy. Towering over six feet with a huge bust and equally large posterior, Lorita accentuated her bizarre stature by extending her immense bosom far out in front and moving her protruding behind with a sashaying, butt-swinging walk designed to attract the attention of any male anywhere.

Lorita was not badly retarded, but no one doubted that something in her head didn't quite mesh—no one except Lorita, that is.

The mentally handicapped demonstrate a great variation in mental capacity as well as personality, but common to most is an awareness that something about them is different. As a consequence many tend to act reticent and uncomfortable in the presence of those considered "normal." Not Lorita. She swung her outsized chest and rear end from side to side wherever she went, talked loudly and tried, with a good deal of success, to be the center of attention.

The Sunday singing program with her obsession, males, in the audience was the perfect place for Lorita to perform.

Every time they had a singing, she begged the supervisors to allow her get up and say something. They had good reason not to trust Lorita in a situation such as this, but one day she either wore Miss Samuel down or caught her in a weak moment. Miss Samuel gave Lorita permission to stand up and speak. In an attempt to maintain control over whatever the unpredictable woman had in mind, however, Miss Samuel handed her a sheet of paper on which she had written a few lines from the Bible. "You read these lines, Lorita," the supervisor told her, "and nothing else. Okay?"

Lorita nodded eagerly, took the paper, sashayed to the front and whirled around to face her audience. "Girls and boys, women and men," she began without a glance at the paper. "I've had this on my mind for a long time—somethin' I need to tell you. There's somethin' gonna get y'all. It's gonna get you sure. It's gonna wrap you round the tree."

Dr. Woodruff was sitting in the front row with his arms folded across his chest. As the uncomfortable audience began to stir and shuffle with unintelligible grunts, wide-eyed stares, and other signs of agitation, he cast a questioning frown at Miss Samuel. The supervisor rolled her eyes and shrugged helplessly.

"What is it, girls? What is it, boys?" Lorita persisted. "What is it gonna wrap you round the tree?"

A boy in the back ventured nervously, "The Devil?"

"No," Lorita answered with wide-eyed fervor. "It's DEATH. It's DEATH. DEATH is gonna get y'all."

The fearful grunts and groans gained volume as great frowns and worry lines gripped the faces of the agitated audience. Miss Samuel leaped to her feet and escorted Lorita from the limelight as Dr. Woodruff's disgusted exit signaled the end of her speaking career.

A court order dated April 24, 1929, committed Della Raye to Partlow. The order described her as an "indigent feeble-minded person," while an admission application listed her age as seven. The starving girl may have been indigent, but her true age, as well as her alleged feeblemindedness, deserves clarification.

No known birth certificate exists to prove Della Raye's age. Her mother, who was not so simpleminded as to be ignorant of her own past, insisted all her life that Della had been born on April 6, 1924, a date that would have made her four at the time she entered Partlow. Five was the minimum age for admission, and her mother knew that too. She explained to Della that her brother, Della's Uncle Richard, had falsified her age in order to have her committed.

Another admission form dated April 26, 1929, two days after the court order, states that Della was "Born in 1923 [June 2 (?)]" and that she was seven at the time. This does not add up; in fact, it is impossible. Had she been born in June of 1923, as the form states, she would have been five at the time of admission, not seven.

Thus Partlow's own figures prove that Della Raye could not have been the age they claimed her to be. Considering that the figures in the institutional records make no sense, it appears that no one was terribly interested in Della's birth date or true age at the time she was committed. Throughout her life she has gone by the birth date her mother told her: April 6, 1924. And as indicated on her driver's license and her children's birth certificates, the state of Alabama has long accepted this date—a date that says she was four at the time of admission.

As to the allegation that Della Raye was feebleminded, several lines of evidence will be shown to address that issue: her patient records from Partlow, including several IQ tests which were calculated incorrectly and artificially lowered; a court instrument at the time of her release (along with Partlow's frenzied reaction to the order); her life accomplishments; and the professional opinion of a state-board-certified psychologist.

For much of her life Della Raye would not understand why she had been committed to Partlow in the first place.

Granted, she had been starving and badly in need of help, but why a mental institution?

Richard personally escorted his two sisters and Della Raye to the gates of Partlow, but court records indicate that a county welfare worker named Frances Woodruff was instrumental in having the three legally committed. Because of the terrible conditions in which Della Raye existed at the time, Mrs. Woodruff wrote Partlow's director and pleaded with him to allow her entry. The letter indicated a genuine concern for her welfare but mentioned nothing of mental incompetence.

In order to have a person committed to an insane asylum, Alabama law required application through a juvenile or probate court judge and verification of mental deficiency by a three-person panel, one of whom had to be a medical doctor. The two adults, Ruby and Dovie, would likely have appeared retarded to many people, but what made it possible to commit a small child such as Della Raye to a mental institution?

The roots of this travesty lay in the rapidly changing medical and social beliefs of the time. The serious study of mental health was just beginning, the field of psychiatry, largely unknown. Country doctors, small-town physicians, medical aids, and welfare workers regularly made life decisions concerning care and treatment of the mentally handicapped.

The fledgling field of mental health was struggling to meld Darwin's theory of evolution with the newly-discovered principles of genetics. Together these two advances seemed to be telling scientists everything they needed to know about heredity, and though both discoveries were tremendously important and would ultimately open doors to medical breakthroughs, as other scientific advances have done in their infancy, they spawned an excess of hope.

The dread of inherited retardation had plagued families for centuries, and still does. With that age-old fear as a backdrop, the newly-gained knowledge of heredity, sorely incomplete in detail, was thought to hold the key—a cure-all for feeblemindedness. Medical professionals, academics, and physicians alike became convinced that retardation was passed down from generation to generation as a single inherited trait, and as hereditarian theories gained acceptance, attitudes toward the feebleminded began to change. Whereas society had generally treated the unfortunates with compassion and tolerance in the past, now these "mental defectives" became responsible for every form of antisocial behavior that plagued the human race. Laziness, thievery, murder, prostitution, and sexual perversion were all the fault of feeblemindedness. And because mental defectives were considered to be universally devoid of morals and sexually promiscuous, they stood accused of spreading crime and immorality through society like a cancer.

A staff physician at a Mississippi state hospital summed up the growing attitude. "It is also well-known that these mental weaklings are very prolific, and when allowed to go at will, that a line of law-breakers, such as murderers, sexual perverts, pyro-maniacs and thieves are brought into the world to become a burden and a menace to the state."

While a misinformed public trembled in the face of a perceived threat that historians would later dub the "Menace of the Feebleminded," fear grew out of proportion, generating a manic rush to solve the problem. The study of eugenics began in earnest.

The so-called "science" of eugenics, a Hitleresque theory of race purification through selective breeding, gained wide acceptance throughout Europe and America during the first half of the twentieth century. Francis Galton, the English scholar who devised the word from the Greek meaning "well-born," wrote in 1883: "We greatly want a brief word to express the science of improving stock . . . especially in the case of man. The word eugenics sufficiently expresses the idea."

As the Menace of the Feebleminded threatened to destroy the human race, the proponents of eugenics rode in to save the day. They were well-meaning scientists who, in their eagerness, led themselves and the field of mental health down a path lined with promises they could not keep. Like Della Raye, thousands of innocents would suffer the consequences.

Historical researchers claimed to have traced unbroken lines of feeblemindedness down through family trees spanning as many as five or six generations. Their good intentions notwithstanding, virtually every hereditary study performed during this period was later shown to be flawed. Future advances would prove the details of genetic inheritance far more complex than the proponents of eugenics assumed, but the zealots were convinced they had found the key to inherited traits, and set about to eradicate mental retardation from the human race. In 1915, several prominent leaders across the nation banded together to do exactly that. "A Committee to Eradicate Feeblemindedness" issued its statement of purpose: "To disseminate knowledge concerning the extension and menace of feeblemindedness, and initiate methods for its control and ultimate eradication from the American people."

Because animal breeders had discovered that certain traits within a herd could be de-emphasized by selective breeding, logic told mental health professionals that the genes responsible for retardation could be wiped out by similar measures. Indeed, the first major paper on human eugenics was presented at a meeting of the American Breeders Association.

Eugenicists indelicately referred to reproduction among the feebleminded as "breeding," and to control this breeding, they turned to the same methods used for cattle and hogs: segregation and isolation for those within institutions, and sexual sterilization for those outside.

Similar methods, though more radical, were being employed in Nazi Germany where Hitler was attempting to eradicate the retarded as well as the entire Jewish race. Retarded citizens were never gassed in this country, as they were by the Nazis, though a few zealots did propose such measures.

In the wake of this misguided revolution in mental health, eugenicists convinced the legislatures in a majority of the forty-eight states that the menace of retardation, along with its attendant degeneracy and immorality, could be wiped from the human race. Nearly every state set about building an institution for the mentally retarded—not for the purpose of caring for them, but for isolating them and preventing their "breeding." Indeed, if the Nazi experiment in race purification hadn't ultimately failed so miserably, the American eugenics movement might not have either.

Back to the question of Della Raye. How could a little girl with no apparent symptoms of retardation be committed to a mental institution? The answer: guilt by association. Della's mother and aunt were considered feebleminded. Regardless of symptoms, or the lack thereof, the flawed theory of inherited traits said she was retarded as well.

Della Raye could have arrived at Partlow reciting Shakespeare and doing long division at the age of four and still been considered feebleminded by the physicians in charge of her future.

Sitting in the dining room watching the other girls eat, Della Raye learned that all patients were not equal. A few of the girls had families on the outside who paid for their stay in Partlow. These girls slept in the same wards with the state patients, and lived and worked by the same schedule, but they wore nicer clothes, had shoes that fit, and ate better food.

Non-state patients ate the same food as the employees; it was better than what we got and there was more of it. One of them would be sitting right across the table from me, eating a heaping plate of food with more seasoning in it than mine and drinking a glass of milk. Oh, how I loved sweet milk, but most of the time I just had a cup of water to drink with my meal.

Della Raye also learned that other patients received letters in the mail and that many had visitors come to see them regularly. Her Uncle Richard had told the institution to bury her on the grounds in case of her death, and since she had no relatives on the outside except him, she would not see one visitor nor receive a single piece of mail for nineteen years.

The church programs and Sunday singings were unique in that both boys and girls were included in the audience. One other form of entertainment included both sexes: dancing. On Saturday nights they would clear the floor in the Schoolhouse and hold a dance for the patients. Two male attendants and their sons provided the music. Everything from the slowest waltzes to the liveliest square dances rang out on banjos, guitars, and fiddles, regular musical fare for much of the South.

Partlow's dances were unique in that boys and girls were not permitted to dance together. Male and female patients sat across the room from each other and no one was supposed to even look at the opposite sex. They alternated dances. First the girls would get up and dance together; then when they sat down, the boys would do the same.

Della found the dancing hilarious. The memory of two boys, clumsily waltzing their way across the floor while stomping on each other's feet still makes her laugh. And whether it was boys or girls on the floor, she especially enjoyed the square dances; Lorita Fricard did the calling.

Lorita was the official caller for all square dances. Up on the stage in front of all the men, she was in her glory. Thrusting her tremendous bosom forward and her ample behind in the opposite direction, Lorita would whirl around and around clapping her hands, stomping her feet and hollering: "Chicken in the bread pan kicking out dough, grab your partner and dosey-do!" Her whirling skirt would stand straight out from her waist as she spun, giving the wide-eyed men a ringside ogle at her long tall legs.

Lorita's brother, a shy, polite fellow, was also a patient. Occasionally he'd cast a fond glance across the room at Della, but when Lorita was up in front calling a dance, her brother sat mortified and stared at the floor.

Lorita was something else. She was so funny up there. I don't know why they didn't stop her, but they always let her do it.

Because mentally handicapped people are often poorly coordinated and may be physically deformed as well, many didn't participate in the dancing. And some couldn't dance for other reasons. Jeannie, a sweet little deaf and dumb girl, couldn't hear the music at all, so she just stood around and grinned while the others danced.

No one cared to dance with Willa Mae Kilpatrick. A cute, skinny little girl who had been abandoned on the steps of a church as a baby, her entire body was covered with eczema. A young couple had taken Willa Mae home for a trial adoption at the age of five or six, but faced with their natural daughter's jealousy, they returned her within a year, turned their backs on her, and relegated her to a life in Partlow.

Bernadette, a terribly sad little girl who might have once thought she was pretty, stood off to the side in her own world, her body limp, her face devoid of expression or care. An only child, she had lost her mother around the age of twelve. After her mother died, Bernadette's father kept her imprisoned in the house and used her sexually until she lost her mind.

Clarine, a stubborn girl who hated the dances, sat on the side of her bed one Saturday night and refused to go. The attendants left Clarine in the ward, but when they got to the Schoolhouse, Miss Samuel asked them where she was. When they told her that Clarine had refused to come, the supervisor barked, "I don't care if she wants to come to the dance or not. Go back and get her and carry her over here."

A few minutes later the dance was interrupted by loud screaming and hollering as several attendants came through the door carrying Clarine, kicking and fighting all the way. "I said I didn't want to go to no dance!" the girl yelled. "I hate the damn things!"

"I don't care what you hate, little girl," Miss Samuel told her. "You're going to come to the dance like everybody else." Then she ordered the attendants to lay Clarine face down on the floor and sit on her back to hold her down.

Even being sat upon by attendants didn't stop her; Clarine continued to holler and disrupt the dance for the rest of the evening. When it ended, Miss Samuel ordered the attendants to give her a stern lesson. "Take her back to the ward and give her a hot enema. That ought to take the fight out of her."

Clarine continued to scream and fight as half a dozen attendants carried her back to the dormitory, through the ward, and into the bathroom. In the bathroom they threw her on the floor, ripped off her clothes, turned her on her stomach, and set about to force an enema tube into her rectum. As the feisty girl continued to struggle, one woman squeezed the liquid bottle to pressurize it while another aimed the tube for its bobbing target. When the tube touched her bottom, Clarine jerked so violently she pulled her head loose from an attendant's grip. Lashing out to bite the person holding the tube, she missed and bit the tube in two instead. As the hot liquid spewed over the cursing attendants, they jumped up and scattered out the bathroom door as if they had violated a nest of hornets.

Clarine continued to scream as the attendants wiped the steaming liquid off their faces, shook their heads in disgust, and left the ward. That ended the dance for that evening, and the enema.

Clarine was as stubborn as a mule. She's the only one I ever thought might have been as stubborn as me.

Della Raye learned to get along with most of the patients during her first year in Partlow, but for those in authority, her stubborn defiance lurked just beneath the surface. Because she had been whipped so many times and never made to cry, they began experimenting with more imaginative forms of punishment.

One day Della made the mistake of sassing Miss Samuel. She thought she'd be in trouble for sure, but to her surprise the supervisor only looked at her narrowly and didn't say a word. That night after she went to sleep, an attendant shook her awake. "Come with me, Della Raye," the woman said. "Miss Samuel's got a little surprise for you."

Della crawled out of bed, sleepily followed the attendant to the end of the ward, and waited while she unlocked the door. Dressed only in her nightgown, she followed the woman across the dark grounds in her bare feet. The night was warm, and as they approached another dormitory, Della Raye could hear piercing screams and moans coming from its open windows. The attendant unlocked the door to the dormitory, locked it behind them, and led her into a ward in which the air hung heavy, a vile space that reeked of sweating bodies and human waste.

The noises she had heard outside had come from this ward. The screams and moans were louder now, and mixed with the sounds of labored breathing, insane muttering, and cursing. Della was in a place she hadn't known existed: the Untidy Ward. In the faint light seeping through the windows, the attendant led her down the center aisle and pointed to an empty bed. "Miss Samuel said for you to sleep here tonight," the woman told her. "She thinks it might teach you something."

A sheet covered the bed, but in the semi-darkness it appeared rumpled and unmade. "Go on. Get in," the attendant told her. As Della Raye crawled into the bed and covered herself, the woman walked away.

As she listened to the maddening sounds of the hell around her and smelled of its foulness, Della became aware of something slick and slimy against her body and legs. She raised the sheet and quickly covered her nose. The vilest smell of all was coming from her bed. She was lying in shit.

Miss Samuel had ordered it: that she be put into a bed which had been fouled by another patient.

While attempting to scoot herself out of the nastiness, Della Raye tucked the sheet tightly around her neck to try and squelch the stink. Then she began to cry. In the midst of all the craziness, the sobs of one little girl went unheard.

The attendant returned the next morning, got Della up, and walked her through the Untidy Ward in her fouled nightgown. As the morning light poured through the windows she could see it all—a living hell that few people had seen or ever wanted to see.

The eyes of a five-year-old were never meant to view the deformed, drooling faces of hideous souls unaware of their own existence, nor to witness their wildly rolling eyes and the jerking spasms of their twisted bodies, but Della Raye took it all in. She walked beside the attendant, stopped and gazed earnestly at the vegetative bodies lying in beds and strapped upright in chairs, looked into the faces of the ones sitting on benches unable to control the shaking of their palsied heads while muttering insanely to no one in particular, and watched those shuffling slowly around the room doing the same.

Before they left the building, the attendant walked Della to the opposite wing and introduced her to another nightmare, one that she would come to know far too well in the future.

"I'm going to show you something else, Della Raye," the woman said. "The Cross Hall. That's where we lock people up when they're bad or when they get real crazy."

She led Della down a dingy hallway to a line of dark, narrow cages that reeked of feces and urine. Each cage—approximately four feet wide by six feet deep—had a heavy wooden door at its front. A large padlock hung from an iron hasp on every one. The upper half of each door consisted of thick wooden bars separated by carved slits an inch wide; the lower half was solid except for a small opening near the floor for passing food trays and slop jars in and out.

Screams, grunts, and insane babbling echoed from the shadowy caves behind the bars. Through the narrow slits Della could see dim, grimy faces peering out of the darkness.

The Cross Hall—an antiquated jail used for restraining violent and unruly patients as well as for punishment—was solitary confinement in its crudest form. Each cell had a thin, straw-filled pallet on the floor for sleeping, an open slop jar for toilet use, and nothing more. Attendants learned to give the cell doors a wide berth as they walked by, because not all inmates used their slop jars. Some preferred to hold their feces in their hand and await an opportunity to sling it through the bars at an unsuspecting passerby.

When Della Raye had seen it all, the attendant asked her, "You want to spend any more nights over here?" She didn't answer. The woman walked Della back to her own ward, shook her head at the attendants there, and left.

The attendants watched with curiosity as Della walked to her bed, removed her reeking nightgown, and went to the shower. When she came back, she put on clean clothes, turned to them and asked, "Can I have some breakfast?"

Besides emphasizing a sense of humor among survivors, psychiatrist Frankl described the powerful role that religion played in the Nazi death camps. "The religious interest of the prisoners," Frankl wrote, "as far and as soon as it developed, was the most sincere imaginable." He painted moving mental pictures to describe the depths of their beliefs:

". . . improvised prayers or services in the corner of a hut, or in the darkness of the locked cattle truck in which we were brought back and forth from a distant work site, tired, hungry, and frozen in our ragged clothing."

Locked in Partlow, Della Raye would discover the power of such faith. One day after enduring yet another tearless beating from an attendant, she sat on the side of her bed in sullen silence. A girl new to the ward walked over and sat down beside her.

"You look like you're having a pretty hard time around here," the girl said.

Her eyes filled with pain and suspicion, Della looked up at the stranger seated beside her. She was twelve, seven years older than Della, and much larger. Her dumpy body matched a round face topped by short brown hair that was parted down the middle. And as if God had not made her plump face plain enough, the girl wore thick, heavy glasses that magnified her eyes out of proportion.

"What's your name?" Della asked.

"My name's Lula," the homely girl said. "Lula Clemons." Her coke-bottle glasses gave her a bug-eyed look that lent a humorous edge to her straightforward countenance, but Della Raye hardly noticed. She saw only warmth and honesty in Lula's magnified eyes, and heard only tenderness in her voice.

"My name's Della Raye," she said, looking dejectedly at the floor as she spoke. "They're always hittin' me and hollerin' at me and stuff like that. I hate it here."

"I know it's hard, honey," Lula said, then surprised her with a question. "What do you know about God, Della Raye?"

Della looked thoughtful for a moment, then answered. "I go to them church things and they sing about God, but I don't know who He is."

"Have you ever heard of the Bible?" Lula asked her.

"No. What's the Bible?"

"It's a big book that tells about God," Lula said.

"I can't read books," Della answered.

"I know you can't, but I can. And I'm gonna read to you about God."

"When you gonna do that?" Della asked.

"Soon, Della Raye, as soon as I can," Lula answered, and reached over and gave Della the first hug she would ever remember.

Della quickly grew attached to Lula, and in the following days stayed close beside her whenever possible. She heard her asking other young girls about God and telling them of her plans to read the Bible to them. Della grew anxious to hear Lula read from this Bible, and asked her continually when it was going to happen.

Just before bedtime one evening, Lula whispered to Della, "After we go to bed I'll wait till they come back and unlock the bathroom door, then I'll come and get you girls up. We'll all go in the bathroom and I'll read to you, but we'll have to be real quiet."

Two hours later, after the night attendant came through and unlocked the door, Lula tiptoed around the ward and woke the girls. Carrying her Bible in her hand, she led them into the darkened bathroom.

Eight little girls in drab nightgowns sat huddled together on the cold, stone floor, holding hands in the darkness and listening to Lula's hushed voice. A single ray of light broke the blackness. Peering dimly down from a tiny window high above, it fell softly on the pages of the open Bible that rested in the girl's hands. Slowly moving the book back and forth in the narrow wand of light as she read, Lula cautioned lowly, "Quiet now. If one of them catches us, we'll be in big trouble."

The little ones listened without a whisper as she read. She told them of paradise, of one who loved them, of one who died for them, of hope. Then, her face the faintest outline beside the wan finger of light, Lula gently closed the Bible. "All right angels, that's all for tonight. Stay quiet, and say a prayer to God before you sleep."

As the other girls slipped silently out the door into the dark ward, the littlest one stopped and hugged her tightly. "I love you, Lula," she whispered.

"I love you too, Della Raye," she said, patting the soft blond curls. "And God does too."

Historians are well aware that more than a few people of normal intelligence ended up in mental institutions during the first half of the twentieth century. Entire families are known to have been committed at times.

Except for Lula Clemons's father, whom she never mentioned, all of her family resided in Partlow—her mother, her sister, an aunt, a niece, and two brothers who lived at the Boys Colony. The true mental status of her family members will never be known, but Della Raye strongly believes that Lula had nothing wrong with her mind. Della remained in contact with Lula all her life, and while she and others will testify that a lifetime in Partlow made Lula weird and somewhat of a character, that should hardly surprise anyone.

Hereditarians of the period believed that most people living at the poverty level were feebleminded, or at least carried the genes for it, and the law allowed any licensed doctor to declare a person mentally incompetent. As the Depression deepened and the agrarian South became engulfed in the cruelest poverty, judges committed more and more people to

Partlow and similar institutions across the region. Physically handicapped children, orphans, and others with problems unrelated to feeblemindedness found their way into asylums. Whether or not the judges actually agreed with the eugenic view of inherited retardation will never be known; some may simply have seen the mental institutions as the only haven available for people who might otherwise starve.

As incoming patients continued to swamp the wards and state funding continued to dwindle, Partlow was forced to look for ways to become even more self-sufficient. To its credit, the institution housed a great number of retarded citizens and homeless children who had nowhere else to turn during impossible economic times, and certainly Partlow cared for them as well as their meager funds would allow. Unfortunately, the demand for free labor made high-grade patients a premium.

Dr. Woodruff, being both the acting director and the only trained physician on staff, had the responsibility of maintaining the physical health of hundreds of patients as well as running the entire operation on a day-to-day basis. And, because Partlow was a mental institution, he also was charged with assessing the mental state of each person under his care. According to records, Dr. Woodruff administered IQ tests from time to time during a patient's tenure.

The IQ test, invented in 1905 by a French researcher named Binet, was first developed as a teaching aid to help identify children in need of special education. Having designed his test for a specific purpose, Binet knew its limitations. He never considered the IQ score to be an accurate measure of inborn intelligence, but simply intended its use as a rough guide to identify mildly retarded children and those with learning disabilities. He did recognize the great potential for its misuse, however, and strongly cautioned against using IQ scores as a scale for ranking subnormal intelligence.

American psychologists saw the same potential and disregarded Binet's warnings. The French may have developed the

IQ test for the improvement of public education, but American professionals quickly recognized its diagnostic utility. Despite disagreement by the man who had conceived the test, they set about using it as a tool to classify the feebleminded.

Binet was suspect of any system that purported to measure an individual's intelligence and assign it a numerical value. Intelligence was not a fixed entity, he insisted, but a pliant quality capable of being developed through education and environment.

Binet may have conceived the IQ and invented a method for testing it, but a leading American psychologist disagreed with his views concerning the nature of intelligence. H. H. Goddard, the influential Director of Research at the Vineland Training School for Feebleminded Girls and Boys in New Jersey, believed intelligence to be a fixed, immovable quantity unaffected by one's background or education. Goddard was one of the leading eugenicists in the nation, and though he would ultimately be proved wrong, at the time he rejoiced in the belief that he had found a way to define intelligence, or a lack thereof, by an absolute number. He defined the three levels of feeblemindedness by the following IQ ranges: idiot, less than 25; imbecile, 25-55; and moron, 55-75. And as physicians had done prior to the advent of IQ testing, Goddard assigned his subjects mental ages as well: idiot, 2 years or less; imbecile, 3 to 7 years; moron, 8 to 12 years.

Some researchers continued to question the precision of the IQ test, but in the growing bandwagon atmosphere, the voices of dissent were lost. Institutional directors such as W. D. Partlow, the outspoken champion and undisputed leader of eugenics in the Deep South, had found a foolproof method for classifying their patients.

An IQ test consisted of performing a series of tasks which correlated with a certain mental age. For example, the first test given Della Raye stated the following requirements for mental age six.

AGE: SIX YEARS
1. Right and Left: R. hand, L. ear, R. eye.
2. Mutilated pictures (3 of 4): eye, mouth, nose, arm.
   (The pictures shown to the patients were commonly simple
   sketches of a person with the listed part missing.)
3. Counts 13 pennies (1 of 2).
4. Comprehension (2 of 3):
   What is the thing to do:
           (a) If it is raining when you start for school?
           (b) If you find that your house is on fire?
           (c) If you are going some place and miss your car?
5. Coins (3 of 4): nickel, penny, quarter, dime.
6. Repeat:
           (a) We are having a fine time. We found a
              little mouse in the trap.
           (b) Walter had a fine time on his vacation.
              He went fishing every day.
           (c) We will go out for a long walk.
              Please give me my pretty straw hat.

A patient who could satisfactorily perform all of these tasks was assigned a mental age of at least six. The same scoring applied if the patient could perform the tasks for mental age seven, eight, and so on.

The test was administered orally, the doctor judging the results subjectively and noting them on the test sheet. He then assigned the patient both a mental age and a numerical IQ score.

The first IQ test in Della Raye's record, dated May 17, 1932, was administered by "L. H. Woodruff, M.D." Her chronological age and test results were listed as:

Chronological age: 9

Mental age: 6 years, 10 months

IQ: 67

In order to arrive at an IQ score of 67, the tester used a mental age of exactly six years—an incorrect calculation. According to the Encyclopedia of Human Behavior, the full six years and ten months should have been used in the formula. Had this mental age been used—the one the tester himself had deduced—Della Raye's IQ would have calculated 76. And, bearing in mind that Della Raye was born in April 1924, she was actually eight at the time of the test.

What does this mean? If the doctor had used her true chronological age and the full mental age indicated by his own testing, he would have calculated Della Raye's IQ at 85, a figure well into the range that is considered "normal."

By today's standards, an IQ score of 70 or above lies within the range of normal intelligence, and modern psychologists readily acknowledge that environment and education, or a lack thereof, can affect an individual's score considerably.

Dr. James Gardiner, a board-certified neuropsychologist who has personally tested more than two thousand patients with varying levels of brain injury and retardation, is familiar with Della Raye's background, her trials, and her life achievements. In his professional opinion, Dr. Gardiner states, her IQ, if tested today, would be "at least above average, and likely greater than 100."

Also according to records, patients were given physical exams every one to two years. Notations under "Family and Personal History" generally included the patient's age, size, health, behavior, and mental diagnosis. The reports varied from a few lines to a long paragraph.

The first entry in Della's record, dated June 21st, 1929, states:
". . . general appearance is good; well developed and nourished; sight and hearing good, . . . face has dull expression."

Two years later, July 9, 1931:
". . . fairly well nourished and developed; quiet, bright and cooperates well; sight and hearing good . . ."

August 15, 1932:
"She has had no illness during the past year and has shown no change mentally or physically, but is getting along well as usual . . . general appearance defective looking . . ."

July 6, 1933:
". . . looks well physically. She has shown no mental change and is doing as well as could be expected for one of her type."

August 1, 1934:
". . . doing as well as could be expected in every way."

May 1, 1935:
". . . growing and developing well and gets along nicely in every way."

February 1, 1936:
". . . general appearance defective looking . . ."

By 1936, seven years after being committed, Della Raye had not yet been diagnosed as a moron, imbecile, or idiot. Apparently, one year her face had had a "dull expression," twice her general appearance had been "defective looking," and another year she was doing as well as could be expected for "one of her type."

The wooden structure known as the Schoolhouse served as a center for many activities, and it actually was a schoolhouse of sorts. Girls and boys considered capable of learning went to school for one hour each day when Della was small, and the sessions were later increased to two hours per day. Girls and boys attended separate classes in the Partlow school, the girls being taught by a woman and the boys by a man. The highest level offered was grade five, with eighteen being the maximum age a patient could attend. The curriculum did offer the patients a bit of reading, writing, and mathematics, but since the prevailing eugenic philosophy said that most of them would remain there all their lives, asylum schools tended to concentrate primarily on teaching the children how to get along within the institution. The merits of punctuality, obedience to authority, teamwork, and respect for others were emphasized over traditional academics.

Partlow did have a teacher that impressed Della Raye. Rena Scott, an energetic young woman in her twenties, taught all grades. Tall, thin, poised, with brown hair worn in tight bangs, Miss Scott was a pretty lady, with the exception of a pock-marked complexion left from childhood.

Although Rena Scott did not have a college degree, she attended university classes at night while teaching at Partlow. And though some of her students could retain virtually nothing and others learned only with great difficulty, Rena did her best to teach the children what she could in the short time the institution allotted her.

School came easy for Della Raye, and she loved to learn. Rena Scott obviously recognized that her intelligence was superior to most of the other students, and she would one day enter the following statement into Della's official record:

> "SCHOOL NOTES: Della Raye does excellent in all phases of her school work. She has completed the fifth grade and could possibly do more advanced work if it were possible to have a more advanced class. She is one of the best girls in occupation, doing excellent work in which she takes a great deal of pride. Her motor ability is above that of the average normal child."

Semi-literate adults—those with only a few years of schooling—are often able to recognize individual words but find it difficult to grasp the meaning of a complete sentence. For such a person to read and comprehend an entire book is virtually impossible.

Della Raye may have learned the rudiments of word recognition in the institutional school, and perhaps how to struggle through a sentence, but she taught herself to read. And she absorbed every single book in Partlow's small library.

Ruby lived in the same building as Della Raye, but on the second floor. Della remained unaware of it, however, and did not see her mother for more than two years after their arrival at Partlow. She doesn't know how the attendants managed to keep them so isolated from each other, but even though the older girls (women) ate along with the younger ones, she never saw Ruby.

As a little girl Della Raye felt lost in a sea of big people.

Many of the big people had seemed weird and funny-looking at first, and some acted very strange. But as she grew accustomed to their company, she learned that most patients were harmless; many were friendly, and some of the strangest treated her with tenderness.

As she grew older and taller, Della learned that she could manipulate most of the other patients and steer them in whatever direction she pleased. But though her intelligence outshone most of theirs, an even more fundamental differ-ence separated her from the others: an unyielding defiance.

After undergoing a certain amount of punishment, most patients learned that a compliant attitude would keep them out of trouble. Take whatever comes your way; do whatever anyone tells you; plod through the day with no concern for your own needs. In the milling, staring crowd, one could forget all about personal preferences. And so life went on for most patients—unchanging and deathly dull—with little punishment.

Not Della Raye. She didn't operate that way, and she often paid a high price for it. She got along well with attendants like Rena Scott or Mama Leonard—those who afforded the patients some measure of dignity—but she hated the ones who wielded authority simply for the sake of wielding it. And she didn't necessarily agree with all the rules either.

Lula watched in horror as Della Raye defied the attendants and refused to back down from any fight. Standing a safe dis-tance down the ward while Della fought and lost many a bloody battle, Lula shook her head and prayed for her stub-born, diminutive friend. Della Raye prayed too, but God seemed to have a hard time keeping her in line.

They were determined to break me, and I was determined they wouldn't. I would have died before I'd shed a tear for them.

One day when Della was seven, she got into a fight with two attendants at the same time. The women took turns yanking her by the hair, slapping her, punching her, and knocking her to the floor. Each time one of them knocked her down, Della would jump back to her feet and fight on. Finally, the attendants stopped in frustration, looking at Della's rumpled hair, swollen face, and reddened, defiant eyes. Then one of them pointed a finger at her and said, "You wait here, little girl. You think you're so damn tough. We'll see about that."

The attendant stomped off the ward, while the other one stood and watched Della. Within minutes the door opened again and the attendant walked in. Ruby was following behind her. Della Raye had not seen her mother in more than two years—not since the day they had arrived at Partlow.

"Mama!" she cried, and started to run toward Ruby. But something in her mother's eyes made her stop.

As she closed the distance between them in a stoop-shouldered shuffling walk, Ruby pointed a threatening finger and said, "Della Raye, these women tell me you ain't been bein' good. You gotta stop that. That ain't no way to get along around here."

"Remember what I told you, Ruby," the attendant threatened. Ruby nodded, and before Della could react, her mother grabbed her in a headlock and began beating her in the face with her fist.

"Mama! Mama! What are you doing?!" Della screamed, jumping around and around in a circle. Ruby spun with her, and slugged her again and again.

"Stop it Mama! Stop beating me!" Della yelled.

When Della Raye began to cry, the attendants grinned with satisfaction. As she screamed hysterically and fought to break loose, Ruby stopped swinging and started to loosen her grip.

"Don't stop yet, Ruby!" one of the women hollered. "She's had this coming for a long time."

Ruby tightened her grip, and the beating resumed. Snot, tears, and flecks of blood flew as she slapped Della Raye hard in the face and slugged her repeatedly in the shoulders and head.

"That's it, Ruby. Get her good!" the attendants shouted gleefully.

Finally it stopped. Ruby released her grip, dropped her arms, and looked at Della sadly. Slump-shouldered,

simple-faced, hollow-eyed Ruby who would do anything anyone told her. She made Della cry. She'd been their ace in the
hole.

Della stood looking at her mother—her chin quivering,
her body shaking, her bloodshot eyes filled with tears and an
unspeakable hurt. Then Ruby seemed to melt. Reaching out
her arms and slouching forward, she pleaded helplessly, "Oh
Della Raye, I'm so sorry."

Della jumped back from her outstretched arms. "Get away
from me!" she screamed.

"But I love you," Ruby said pitifully, reaching for her again.

"No you don't!" Della screamed. "You don't love me. And I
don't love you either. I hate you!" Della stood wiping her tears
and her bleeding nose as the smug attendants led her mother
away.

Every night since she had learned to pray, she had prayed
for her freedom. That night as she lay in bed, bruised and
sore, Della Raye folded her small hands and looked upward.
"Jesus, please help me hang on till I can get big enough to
take up for myself. Then if I have to stay here, maybe I won't
mind it so bad."

CHAPTER FOUR

Heaven and Hell

Near the end of 1929, the year Della Raye arrived, Partlow's patient population reached 332. The state appropriation to feed, clothe, and care for each one was a meager three dollars per week, far below the national average. By 1940 the population would grow to 714 and the weekly appropriation would rise to four dollars per patient. And as the board of trustees pointed out that year, this figure fell far short of the seven dollars or more that other states were providing for their mental patients.

As new patients continued to arrive through the 1930s, somehow the burgeoning population had to be contained. W. D. Partlow had virtually no time to practice medicine, but he honed his business skills and found innovative ways to cope with the growing problem.

The Boys Colony, having begun with an initial acquisition of eighteen hundred acres, was originally established to provide an inexpensive source of food for the institution. By setting aside a portion of the three-dollar weekly patient allotment, Dr. Partlow purchased additional land, expanded the farming operation to nearly three thousand acres, and began raising cash crops. Using the income from cash crops and continuing to withhold money from the patient allotments, Dr. Partlow funded three new dormitories during the 1930s—one at the Boys Colony and two at Partlow. Small state appropriations and a federal grant helped a bit, but the resourceful director paid for most of the construction with funds he had raised himself. Bryce Hospital had its own farm colony as well, and Dr. Partlow financed two new buildings on its grounds using the same methods.

The deplorable conditions within mental institutions had been noted as early as 1769, the year William Buchan described the famous English asylum known as Bedlam. The candid doctor stated that such places were "far more likely to make a wise man mad than to restore a madman to his senses."

If one looked past the barbed wire fence and the bars on the gate, on the outside Partlow appeared calm, controlled, and quiet. Within the massive buildings, however, inside the hopelessly crowded wards, Della Raye and hundreds of others passed every hour of every day in a constant clamor. Patients wandered aimlessly, bumping and brushing against each other with every move. A sea of humans, their senses dulled beyond care, milling about like a school of fish—individuals moving in circles, crisscrossing, or pacing the length of the ward, but the crowd itself going nowhere. Some jabbered endlessly while others shouted nonsense and obscenities into the ears of their closest neighbors; some sat in corners or leaned against walls; some perched on the backs of benches, like chickens on fences; and some sat constantly, maddeningly, rocking back and forth for hours. The din of too many people, living in too small of a space, never ceased.

Della's Aunt Dovie lived in the high-grade adult ward with Ruby. Dovie was hopelessly addicted to snuff; whoever controlled her snuff controlled her. She had the same long, narrow face as her siblings Richard and Ruby, but Dovie was less complacent than her sister and given to fits of anger. Threatening to withhold her snuff usually took care of the anger, and because she behaved reasonably well under supervision and showed compassion for the little ones, Dovie spent her life caring for the low-grade children in the Untidy Ward.

I have fond memories of Dovie. She was kind to me. She wasn't very smart but I always felt that she had more common sense than my mother did.

Both Dovie and Ruby were classified as imbeciles. Each had a measured IQ near 40, and neither could read or write. While Ruby went along with everything and seldom spoke harshly to anyone, Dovie had definite opinions about her sister, which she never missed a chance to air.

"You always was oversexed, Ruby," Dovie would yammer for the thousandth time. "Why, you're nothin' but an old whore," she'd continue as Ruby pretended not to hear. The two of them lived in the same ward and maintained that one-sided nagging relationship for most of their lives.

Plodding, complacent Ruby worked long hours in the kitchen, one of the hardest jobs at Partlow. "Get your stupid ass to work, Ruby Rogers!" Betty Myers would yell. "We got a lotta damned mouths to feed." And Ruby would dutifully bend to her task. Over the years Myers would drive, curse, and abuse Ruby until her back was permanently bowed from lifting hundred-pound sacks of flour, carrying heavy containers to and from the storage room, and mixing barrel-size cauldrons of soups, stews, and vegetables seven days a week.

Della's older brother, Frank, had been living in the county almshouse at the time she and her mother and Aunt Dovie were committed. A few months after their arrival, Frank also came to Partlow. He was eleven at the time, six years Della's senior, and was sent to work at the Boys Colony. An easy-going lad of medium height and build, Frank was thin-faced like his mother and even more simpleminded.

Frank wore bib overalls every day, his personal preference, and seemed to epitomize a statement once made by a mental patient at Bryce: "A crazy man and a wheelbarrow must have been made for each other." Frank learned to count to four but could master nothing higher, and knew the purpose of a clock but never learned to tell time. He didn't worry about such things, though; he loved his work at the Colony and little else mattered. Simple responsibilities such as milking cows and gathering eggs became Frank's challenges in life, and he took them seriously. Of course, the punishment, exacted by the supervisors if he didn't do well, provided an added incentive to work hard at his job.

Dickie Jr., the younger brother who had been torn from Ruby's arms the day they were committed, eventually came to Partlow as well, but not until seven and a half years had passed. Although he was so badly retarded he could not speak, somehow Dickie ended up in a foster home during those years. He had lived near a school where he had started bothering the children, taking things from them, and generally disrupting the neighborhood until something had to be done with him.

It was 1936 when Dickie Jr. showed up at Partlow; he was ten. His face didn't appear as long and thin as most of the family's, and though virtually incapable of taking an IQ test and shy to the extreme, Dickie seemed a likable guy. Photos in his record show the smiling face of a simple little fellow, obviously happy to be posing. During one of his physical exams, the doctor wrote: "Dick comes right up to me and pats me on the knee and he seems to be in good health."

Though classified as an idiot with an IQ below 20, and described as a "mouth-breather" who ate everything with a spoon and never talked, Dickie Jr. could perform simple tasks such as hoeing a garden or mopping a floor. After several years at Partlow, he was transferred to the Boys Colony with Frank, where he also wore bib overalls and would spend the rest of his life doing menial tasks.

Sometime during Dickie's middle age, a doctor discovered that he could speak in simple one- and two-word phrases. When the doctor asked him what he did at the Colony, Dickie smiled shyly and told him he worked with the "hoe bunch."

Nobody ever said where the "Junior" in Dickie's name came from; everybody in the family just called him that. It may be a terrible thing to say, but I've often wondered if Uncle Richard might have been those boys' father.

Many of the patients were related. Records for one year in the 1940s show that one hundred seventy-seven patients had at least one relative in Partlow. Some, like Della Raye, had several relatives there. Though most of the related patients lived in separate wards and many hardly knew each other, for some reason Partlow instituted "family get-togethers" when Della was a child. A few times each year, regardless of age, gender, or mentality, they would assemble all the members of a family and allow them to sit together and visit for one hour.

Frank and Dickie Jr. would be driven in from the Colony, and along with Della Raye, Ruby, and Dovie, ushered into the Schoolhouse and seated in a circle of chairs while attendants hovered in the background. Then for an hour Frank would carry on about his beloved cows, pigs, and chickens; Ruby would sit quietly while Dovie called her an old whore. Dickie Jr. would sit limply in his chair and smile stupidly at a group of people he didn't recognize, and Della would glower at her mother for the beatings she had given her.

And the attendants continued to bring Ruby to Della Raye's ward to give her the beatings. At their insistence, Ruby would pound her unmercifully; and when they allowed her to stop, she would always reach for Della and tell her that she loved her. But though her mother was the only one who could ever hurt Della badly enough to make her cry, her reaction to this affectionate aftermath never changed.

"No! Don't you touch me," Della Raye would yell at her mother. "And don't tell me you love me either. You wouldn't beat me if you loved me. I hate you!"

That was so awful. I've always thought if God was ever displeased with me about anything, it would be over the way I felt toward my mother during those years.

Della Raye had reached the in-between years: not a little girl any more but not yet a teenager either. She had defiantly fought the system from the age of four and found comfort in the support of two important beings: God and Lula Clemons. She still had them both—Lula to pray for her and God to protect her. Then Della began to worry over something concerning God.

She had never been baptized, and she'd heard that people who hadn't been baptized could not be forgiven for their sins. She knew she would never be baptized in Partlow, and feared that if something happened to her—if somehow she died—she wouldn't make it to Heaven.

The fear of dying a sinner didn't change Della's attitude or keep her out of trouble, but it made her feel even more alone. What if the God whom she loved would not welcome her into Paradise? At night when she prayed for her freedom, she would ask, "Lord, how will I ever be with you in Paradise if I can't get baptized?"

Then one day she received an unexpected gift, a Bible. A patient in the adult female ward was going blind, and now that she could no longer read, she wanted Della Raye to have her bible. The woman's name, Rosa Lee, was printed on the front cover. It was surely her most prized possession.

Rosa Lee had chosen her recipient well. A Bible of her very own was the greatest gift Della Raye could imagine. She treasured it, protected it, and read it every day. She marveled at every word in it, words that she would come to know by heart and learn to live by as few ever do. And one day while reading of the crucifixion, she found her answer to the question of baptism.

Jesus told that thief on the cross next to him: "This day you will be with me in Paradise." I knew that old thief could not have been baptized and if he could go to Heaven, then I could too.

Church and community organizations sometimes contributed used refrigerators and other badly-needed items to Partlow. Della Raye, Lula, and the other girls often participated in plays that Rena Scott directed and were delighted when they received a piano for the Schoolhouse. Willa Mae Kilpatrick learned to play it and provided musical accompaniment for their productions.

Della Raye and Lula performed in most of the plays. She recalls a play in which Lula portrayed an old woman, down on her hands and knees, wearily scrubbing a floor. The very title of the play, *Over the Hills to the Old Folks Home,* projected a dreary mood. And whether it was done purposely or subconsciously, the negative aura seemed to reflect the general outlook of their lives.

I loved the plays. I was skinny as a rail, I had black freckles, and I knew I wasn't pretty. I didn't normally feel like we had any dignity at all in there, but I loved acting in those plays.

You know how you can lie in bed at night when you're a child and imagine things you'd like to be? I dreamed that someday, somehow, I would be an actress.

Besides striving to express themselves through acting, Della Raye and Lula wrote poems and prayers. Over the years they filled several notebooks with their work. One of Lula's poems tells the poignant story of a little boy named Tommy, and between the lines, it tells much of her. Written by an incarcerated teenager with practically no schooling, the poem reflects a view from the lower rungs of the ladder of life, as well as her overwhelming faith in a savior that one day would deliver them into Paradise.

Tommy's Prayer
by Lula Clemons

In a dark and dismal alley where the sunshine never came,
Dwelt a little boy named Tommy, sickly, delicate, and lame.
He had never yet been healthy, but had lain since he was born,
Dragging out his weak existence, hopeless and forlorn.

He was six years old, little Tommy, 'twas just five years ago;
Since his drunkard mother dropped him, and the babe was crippled so.
He had never known the comfort of a mother's tender care,
But her cruel blows and curses made his pain still worse to bear.

There he lay within the cellar from morning until night,
Cursed, neglected, starved, ill treated, no one to make his dull life right.
Not a single friend to have him, not a single thing to love,
For he knew not of the Savior, nor of Heaven up above.

'Twas a quiet summer evening, and the alley was so still;
Tommy's little heart was singing, and he felt so lonely till
Up the quiet alley, coming inward from the street,
Came the sound of someone singing, sounding oh, so clear and sweet.

Eagerly did Tommy listen as the singing softly came;
Oh, he wished he could see the singer, how he wished he was not lame.
Then he called and shouted loudly, till the singer heard the sound.

'Twas a maid rough and rugged, hair unkempt and naked feet;
All her garments torn and ragged, her appearance far from neat.
"So you called me," said the maiden, "wonder what you want of me?
Most folk call me Singing Jessie, what may your name chance to be?"

"My name's Tommy, I'm a cripple, and I want to hear you sing;
For it makes me feel so happy, sing me something, anything."
And then Jessie answered, smiling, "I can't stay here very long;
But I'll sing a hymn to please you, what I call the Glory Song."

So she sang to him of Heaven, pearly gates, and streets of gold,
Where the happy angel children are not starved or nipped with cold,
But where happiness and gladness never can decrease nor end,
But where Jesus reigns eternally, where time will never end.

Oh, how Tommy's eyes did glisten and took in every word;
As it fell from Singing Jessie, was it true what he had heard?
And so anxiously he asked her, "Is there really such a place?"
And a tear began to trickle down his pale little face.

"Tommy, it's up above the sky;
And if you will love your Savior, you will go there when you die."
Then said Tommy, "Tell me Jessie, how can I the Savior love,
When I'm down in this old cellar, and he's up in Heaven above?"

The little ragged maiden, who had heard at Sunday school,
All about the way to Heaven and the Christian's golden rule,
Taught the little cripple, Tommy, how to love and how to pray;
Then she sang a song of Jesus, kissed his cheek, and went away.

Tommy lay within the cellar, which had grown so dark and cold,
Thinking all about the children in the streets of shining gold.

And he minded not the darkness of that damp and chilly room;
For the joy in Tommy's bosom could get rid of the deepest gloom.

Oh, if I could only see it, thought the cripple as he lay;
Jessie said that Jesus listens, so I think I'll try to pray.
So he put his hands together and he closed his little eyes;
And in wonder deep in earnest, sent a message to the skies.

Gentle Jesus please forgive me, as I didn't know before,
That you cared for little children who are weak and very poor.
And I never heard of Heaven till that Jessie came today,
And told me all about it so I thought I'd try to pray.

You can see me can't you Jesus? Jessie told me that you could;
And I somehow must believe it, for it seems so true and good.
Then she told me if I loved you I would see you when I die,
In the bright and happy Heaven that is up beyond the sky.

Lord I'm only just a cripple and I'm no use here below;
For I heard my mother whisper she'd be glad if I would go.
I'm so cold and lonely sometimes, and I feel so hungry too;
Can't you take me blessed Jesus, up to Heaven along with you?

Oh I'd be so good and patient, and I'd never cry or fret;
And your kindness to me Jesus, I would surely not forget.
I would love you all I know of and I'd never make a noise;
Can't you find me just a corner, where I could watch the other boys?

Oh I think you'll do it Jesus, something seems to tell me so;
For I feel so good and happy, and I sure do want to go.
How I'd love to see you Jesus, and the children all so bright;
Come and fetch me won't you Jesus? Come and fetch me home tonight."

Tommy slowly ceased his prayer, he had told his hearts desire;
Then he waited for an answer till his head began to tire.
So he turned toward his corner and lay huddled in a heap,

Closed his little eyes so gently and was quickly fast asleep.

Oh I wish that every scoffer could have seen his little face,
As he lay there in the corner of that dark and dirty place.
For his countenance was shining like an angel fair and bright;
And it seemed to fill the cellar with a holy Heavenly light.

He had only heard of Jesus from a ragged singing girl;
He might well have wondered, doubted till his head began to whirl.
But he took it as she told it, and believed it then and there,
Simply trusting in the Savior and his kind and loving care.

In the morning when his mother came to wake her crippled boy,
She discovered that his features wore a look of perfect joy.
And she shook him somewhat roughly, but the cripple's face was cold;
He had gone to join the children in the streets of shining gold.

Tommy's prayer had soon been answered, and the angel death had come,
To remove him from the cellar to his bright and shining home,
Where sweet comfort, joy, and gladness never can decrease nor end,
But where Jesus reigns eternally, where time will never end.

In an effort to help the high-grade girls learn manual skills and become more productive workers, Partlow held craft classes a few evenings a week. Maggie Williams, the kindest attendant Della knew, taught the classes. The girls lovingly called her Miss Maggie, and though they used her first name, no one ever disallowed it. A trim lady in her mid-thirties, dignified but not distant, Miss Maggie patiently strove to teach the girls everything they were capable of learning, and she always had time for a kind word. Della Raye excelled at manual arts, and under Miss Maggie's tutelage she learned to sew, crochet, embroider, and knit. She and another girl once crocheted a large bedspread, which Partlow proudly showcased to visitors to demonstrate their patients' accomplishments.

When the craft class ended in the evening, Miss Maggie

would escort the girls back to their dormitory and sometimes stay and help put them to bed. They loved it when she lingered at bedtime. At the girls' urging, she would lead them in a prayer before they got into bed or sing them a hymn before they went to sleep. One evening Miss Maggie had them all kneel beside their cots and ask God to bless something in their lives. One by one, the girls took turns praying aloud. Most of their blessings were bestowed upon favorite people: "God bless Miss Maggie"; "God bless my friend, Alice"; "God bless Mama Leonard." Some of the simpler girls looked around for ideas and ended up saying things such as: "God bless the window" or "God bless my bed."

A sincere little retarded girl had seen a maintenance man repairing a toilet earlier that day. When her turn came, she knelt in strained silence for a long moment, then beamed and said proudly, "God bless the toilet man." Miss Maggie bit her lip, then moved on to the next girl.

One night after the lights went out, I heard a girl crying in the ward. That wasn't unusual, but then I heard Maggie Williams talking to her, consoling her. She was the only employee I ever heard do something like that.

Della Raye made other friends besides Lula and Maryanne, but she chose them carefully. Mary Simprish, an innocent girl attracted by Della's confidence, would remain her friend for as long as she lived. Mary's parents had died, her family had been torn apart, and she had lost track of her siblings. Tall, dark-haired, and slightly stooped, Mary's tentative brown eyes reflected a vulnerability that seemed to invite tragedy at every turn of her life.

When a petite blond named Grace Wright came to Partlow at age eleven, the beautiful girl and Della immediately became friends. They laughed and joked often together, and Della Raye sensed that Grace possessed a keen mind. The stunning girl's eyes, however, did not laugh, and beneath the surface there lurked a quiet sadness that Della could not fathom.

Something about her relationship with Grace puzzled Della Raye. Whenever she and Grace were seen together, Della noticed that an attendant would often find a reason to separate them. Unbeknown to the girls, Millie Hennessy had instructed the attendants to keep Grace away from Della. One day the supervisor walked by the two of them and said, "You go on and find something else to do, Della Raye. You don't have to be hanging around with Grace all the time."

Later that day Della asked her, "Grace, why are they always trying to keep us apart?"

Grace's eyes dropped. "They think I'm not good enough to be your friend," she said.

"Not good enough? Why not?" Della asked. "Why shouldn't I be your friend?"

Grace was nearly too embarrassed to speak. "Because I had a baby," she said, looking at the floor.

"A baby!" Della replied. "You had a baby?"

"Yeah, I had a baby, when I was ten years old. I was one of the youngest mothers anybody ever heard of in the whole United States. It was in all the papers and everything. That's why Miss Hennessy don't want you to be friends with me."

"A baby!" Della exclaimed again. "My Lord, where is it?"

"I don't know," Grace said. "They took it away from me and put me in here, and nobody even comes to see me now. Lord, I miss that baby somethin' awful. I don't even know if it was a boy or a girl, but I think about it all the time." She covered her face and began to sob.

Della reached her arms around the distraught girl and held her. "That's okay, Grace," she said softly. "It doesn't matter what anybody says. You're my friend."

Neither Della Raye nor Grace had ever heard the New Year's bells; so one New Year's eve, they decided to stay awake until midnight and listen for them. After the night attendant turned out the lights, Grace crept out of her bed, sneaked across the ward, and sat down on the floor near the head of Della's bed. "If we don't talk I won't be able to stay awake," she said quietly.

The girls whispered in the dark until they heard the heavy footstep of the night attendant, Mama Dalton, coming through the door. Middle-aged, short, fat, and miserably plain, Mama Dalton not only had a sour disposition, but also had a mean temper. Humiliated at having lost her husband to a younger woman and bitter at being reduced to working as an attendant, she took out her anger on the patients.

Grace huddled in the dark against the wall as Mama Dalton walked past them, but something in the shadows caught her eye. The big woman switched on her flashlight and asked gruffly, "Grace, what're you doin' outta your bed?"

"Me and Della Raye want to hear the New Year's bells," Grace said.

"What's that got to do with you bein' down here by her bed?" the woman asked.

"We're trying to keep each other awake till midnight, Mama Dalton," Della Raye explained.

"Well, you'll just have to keep your ownselves awake," she told them, and ordered Grace to return to her own bed.

A few minutes after Mama Dalton left to continue her rounds, Grace sneaked back and the girls began whispering again. Earlier than they guessed, Mama Dalton returned and caught them a second time. Della Raye knew the corpulent woman had a cruel nature, but for some reason she didn't seem as angry as Della might have expected. And evidently she wasn't; she simply made Grace go back to her own bed again.

Shortly before midnight, after Grace had sneaked back to Della's bed a third time, Mama Dalton walked in again, this time with a paper sack in her hand. "Hey girls, come with me," she said. "I've got somethin' for you." Puzzled at the unexpected invitation, the girls followed her to the door of the attendants' bathroom where they stopped. The bathroom was off-limits to patients.

Unlike the lights in the patient bathroom, which were turned off at night, those in the attendants' bathroom were left on. "Come on in," Mama Dalton told the girls. "It's okay." They followed her inside where the woman opened up the sack and revealed a stack of sandwiches and cookies. "You girls want some goodies to eat?" she asked.

They glanced at each other quizzically, then nodded and said, "Sure." Leaving them both eating happily, Mama Dalton walked out and locked the bathroom door behind her.

Several minutes later, the woman returned and unlocked the door. "Did you get it all ate?" she asked. The girls smiled and nodded approvingly. "Okay then, go on and get back in bed," she said.

As they were leaving the bathroom, Della Raye asked the obvious. "Mama Dalton, why did you give us that food?"

"Did y'all hear the New Year's bells?" the woman said with a sly grin.

Then they remembered. The girls hadn't been able to hear outside noises from the bathroom, and they had lost track of time.

"Did you do that just to keep us from hearing those bells?" Della Raye asked. The woman smirked and laughed cruelly. The girls were stunned; they hadn't heard the New Year's bells after all.

Mama Dalton laughed at them again and said, "Go on and get in your beds now, girls, and stay in them."

Grace and I got off easy. Mama Dalton was a cruel, vulgar person, and she never let anybody have any dignity.

A twelve-year-old girl named Joanie made the mistake of giving Mama Dalton a flippant answer one evening. "All right, Miss Smart Mouth!" the big woman barked. "I'll teach you to mess with me. Get them clothes off!"

"What did you say?!" Joanie asked in disbelief.

"You heard me," Mama Dalton said, pointing a threatening finger in her face. "I said get them damn clothes off, now!" With a ward full of girls watching, Joanie slowly removed her dress, then bent over to take off her shoes. "All of them. Take everything off," the woman ordered. "Strip yerself naked."

As her chin began to quiver, Joanie reached behind her back and slowly removed her little bra. She hesitated a moment, then pulled down her panties. Her face glowing red with embarrassment, she tried to cover herself with her hands. "No, don't cover yerself up," Mama Dalton chided. "Show us what you got, Miss Smarty." Joanie dropped her hands limply to her sides, tears trickling down her cheeks.

"How damn smart you feel now, little girl?" the strutting woman asked. Della Raye and several others turned away in embarrassment.

"Don't turn your heads," Mama Dalton shouted. "Y'all take a close look at Miss Smart Mouth. Here, I'm gonna give you a good look." With that, the attendant grabbed Joanie roughly and threw her to the floor on her back.

"No!" Joanie screamed, and began wailing loudly. With an evil grin, the attendant took hold of her legs and raised them straight up above her body.

Standing with an ankle in each hand, Mama Dalton spread Joanie's legs apart, looked around and barked at the horrified girls. "All right y'all, come up here and get yerself a good look. All of you. March right up here and take a look at what she's got."

As Joanie lay on her back, rolling her head from side to side and sobbing, Mama Dalton held her legs apart and made the girls walk by and look down at her exposed crotch. Several of them were crying as they passed.

When every girl had taken her mandatory look, Mama Dalton dropped Joanie's legs on the floor, stood with her hands on her hips, and looked around coolly. "All right, let that be a lesson to y'all. Any of you try and mess with me, you'll get the same. Understand?"

They understood.

W. D. Partlow possibly wielded more authority than any other institutional director in the nation; on his order alone, a patient could be sterilized. For many years, every patient released from Partlow was surgically sterilized before they left. In 1935, however, the governor of Alabama put a stop to this routine. Dr. Partlow, ever the avid eugenicist, had lobbied heavily in the state legislature and pushed through a sterilization bill that would have become the most liberal in the nation. The bill had passed in both the senate and the house, but after considerable soul-searching, Governor Bibb Graves vetoed it. Voicing his strong beliefs concerning the involuntary sterilization of women, the governor halted the grisly practice in Alabama forever, with this moving statement:

> "We know that the enforcement of the provisions of this bill as to girls and young women will entail major operations upon many thousands. Those who will die are innocent and pure, have committed no offense against God or man, save that in the opinion of experts they should never have been born."

The governor's veto may have stopped the sterilizations, but the unrepentant director answered the rebuff by tightening Partlow's release policy. Fewer were released from the institution after that, though on occasion a girl would still be allowed to leave. In most cases the released patient was only mildly retarded or not at all, and then could leave only in the custody of a parent or another close relative who agreed to sign them out.

Maudie, a girl Della's age, told her excitedly one day, "Guess what, Della Raye? I get to go home! My folks are gonna come and get me and take me home with them."

"Oh, Maudie," Della Raye said, "that's wonderful. No wonder you're so excited."

"I am!" Maudie replied. "Dr. Woodruff said they was comin' tomorrow. I can't hardly wait till they get here!"

When Della told her goodbye the following day, Maudie was so ecstatic she could hardly speak. "Bye, Della Raye," she said with a huge wave. "I hope you get out someday too."

"So do I," Della thought, walking back into the oppressive ward, "but I've got no people out there who care about me."

Della Raye thought of Maudie often in the weeks following

her departure. She could just see her running and playing with neighborhood kids, sitting quietly with her parents at night, going downtown with her mother, and laughing, laughing, laughing. Maudie was one of the lucky ones.

Then one day Della glanced down the ward, and there stood Maudie. After a moment of shocked silence, she said, "Maudie!" and started toward her. But when Maudie dropped her eyes and turned her back, Della Raye stopped and thought better of bothering her. For several days she watched Maudie mope around the ward—silent, dejected, alone. Finally one evening when Maudie was sitting on the edge of her bed staring at the floor, Della ventured her direction and quietly sat down beside her. Both sat looking at the floor a while, then Della broke the silence. "How come you're back, Maudie?"

Maudie answered in a lifeless voice. "It didn't work," she said. "It just didn't work."

"What didn't work?" Della asked.

"Nothin' did," Maudie answered, her voice quavering. "They made fun of me. They teased me and made fun of me," she said, her fists tightening and tears welling in her eyes.

"Who did?" Della Raye asked.

"All of them!" Maudie cried. "The kids. They called me names, called me crazy, run after me callin' me that crazy girl from Partlow." She broke down completely. Leaning on Della's shoulder, she talked through great, racking sobs. "I couldn't stand it. Nobody wanted to play with me. They'd just wait for me to come out so they could laugh at me and call me names. It was awful. I got to where I hated them, and I just stayed in the house and cried most of the time. Maybe I am crazy; it seemed like it was better to come back here after all."

Della Raye wrapped an arm around her shoulders. "I'm sorry, Maudie," she said. "I'm really sorry."

Della was more than sorry about Maudie's plight; she was bewildered, confused, and afraid. What had gone wrong? The idyllic life she had visualized her friend living on the outside hadn't happened. Instead of playing with her, the neighborhood kids had taunted her unmercifully, making her want to return to Partlow. Maudie had gotten the chance they all dreamed of, and now the girl would be afraid to ever try it again. She spent the rest of her life in the institution.

Della Raye loved to watch the movies on Thursday nights, but she also loved to talk. More often than she felt she deserved, Della got posted for talking during meals and was then forbidden to watch the Thursday-night movie. One week she had been especially anxious to see an animated cartoon titled "Bugs in Love." She remembered talking a little in the dining room, and maybe more than once the other girls at her table had frowned and tried to shush her; but she prayed that she hadn't been caught.

Thursday evening after supper the girls lined up and marched to the Schoolhouse to see the movie. After they sat down, an attendant stood in front and called out the names of the ones who had been posted. They were told to leave and gather outside, where they would be marched back to the ward. Della Raye walked to the back of the room when she heard her name called, but instead of going outside, she ducked in among the coats hanging on a rack near the door. She planned to hide there and sneak back in after the movie started, but her quickly-improvised plan failed. Myrna Free, the attendant in charge of assembling them outside, went back in and found her.

"Come on, Della Raye," Miss Free said. "You got posted, and you have to go back with the others." Della marched to the ward in a silent rage. Once inside, she ran and flopped on her bed and began beating her fists and screaming.

Myrna Free was a quiet woman who seldom talked to patients; to Della she had always seemed neutral, neither nice nor mean. "Now Della," Miss Free said in answer to her tantrum, "you knew you'd get posted if you talked in the dining room. You just can't get away with that."

"It's not fair!" Della Raye screamed. "I tried not to talk. And

I prayed all week. I told God how bad I wanted to see that movie. He's not fair; He didn't even listen."

"There's no sense in acting like that," Miss Free said.

"I prayed I'd get to see it," Della raved. "I hate God. I hate him!"

"Oh no, Della, you don't hate God," Miss Free said with concern. "You should never talk like that about God."

"Maudie prayed to get out and go home," Della replied. "But when she did He didn't help her. Why'd He make her come back here?"

"Sometimes we can't know why He does things the way He does," Miss Free said. "Don't hate God, Della Raye. He's all you've got."

Almost a teenager now, Della Raye had grown into an odd mixture of kindness, loyalty, and defiance. With those who treated her fairly, she had always cooperated; with those who didn't, she continued to fight. She loved the kind ones like Mama Leonard, though once she feared she might have turned the woman against her.

Mama Leonard had always been known for her kindness, but many of the girls felt that she favored certain ones, "pets," that hung close to her and seemed to garner special attention. The big woman had every other Monday off, and before each one, she told the girls she'd bring them a piece of candy from town if they were good. Della Raye looked forward to the candy, and tried especially hard to behave around Mama Leonard.

On Saturday mornings the girls sometimes played softball, the only sport Della really enjoyed. One morning when Mama Leonard was supervising the game, Della took off her sweater and stowed it and some other personal items under a bush. While she was playing in the outfield, Della saw one of Mama Leonard's pets walk over to the bush and pick up all of her things except the sweater. The girl waited until Della became distracted by a play, then carried her belongings off and hid them.

When the inning changed and she left the outfield, Della Raye confronted the girl. "Where'd you put my stuff?" she demanded.

"What stuff?" the girl asked innocently.

"You know what I'm talking about," Della said. The girl shook her head and denied any knowledge of it. Della Raye clenched a fist, swung a roundhouse to the girl's chin, and knocked her to the ground. The girl grabbed her face and began writhing on her back and squalling loudly. The melee brought Mama Leonard on a run.

"What's going on here?" the woman hollered.

"Della slugged me!" the girl wailed.

"Is that true, Della Raye?" Mama Leonard asked. "Did you hit her?"

"Yes I did," Della replied. "She stole my things and hid them."

"Shush that racket," Mama Leonard told the girl on the ground. "Did you steal Della's things?" She didn't answer. "If you took her stuff you get yourself up from there and go get it," the woman ordered.

The girl stood up, sheepishly went and got Della's things, and brought them back.

"All right," Mama Leonard said. "Let's play ball."

I thought she might hold that against me, might even whip me, but Mama Leonard didn't even report it. And the next Monday she brought my candy.

For years I'd been praying to get big enough that people would leave me alone, but when I did get bigger nothing changed—and I got mean.

As Della Raye grew stronger, her altercations with employees ceased to be one-sided. During an argument in the ward, an attendant lost her patience, slugged Della in the jaw, and knocked her to the floor. Della came up swinging, landing a blow that sent the startled woman reeling backward several feet. A second attendant jumped in and Della fought her too, but though both women beat her viciously, they could not put her down. After absorbing several jolting blows, the women stopped swinging and backed away.

With eyes blazing from her swelling face, Della Raye jabbed a finger at the bruised attendants. "Don't you go get my mother either," she said. "That's not going to work any more. I'll fight her if I have to."

The fight had gone far enough for the attendants. They walked away, and never again brought Ruby to do their dirty work. Instead they punished Della Raye by sending her to work in the Untidy Ward.

Every morning after breakfast, she walked to the low-grade building and into Hell. In a place where deaths resulted from such revolting maladies as "Epileptic Convulsion," "Diarrhea in an Idiot," and "Exhaustion Due to Idiocy and Malformation," she changed fouled beds, scraped feces from beneath the bodies of bed-ridden idiots, fed and bathed people unaware of her presence, and strapped the badly crippled and deformed into chairs to hold them upright for the day.

The tight binding covering some patients' hands had to be changed—the ones who would inflict wounds upon themselves if allowed to. Jagged scars marked their faces and bodies from having ripped open their skin with their own fingernails. They were strapped into wooden chairs, their hands and forearms bound with soft cloth, and tied firmly to the arm of the chair. There they sat, often in their own waste.

The bully, Mama Herman, worked in the Untidy Ward along with her cousin Fanny. Fanny Herman was middle-aged like Mama Herman, but to the good fortune of her patients, Fanny was her cousin's opposite. Skinny, cheery, and efficient, Fanny treated the untidy patients as humans—as if she considered them real people who possessed souls.

Mama Herman was an unfeeling giant. Perched atop her four-hundred-pound frame, her square, bulbous head looked even larger with its shortly-cropped brown hair dangling straight down like the strings of a mop. Standing in the middle of the ward with her hands on her hips, peering around narrowly through the piggy eyes of a predator, Mama Herman was a patient's worst nightmare. She marched around the ward shouting orders, shoving patients out of her way, and picking up the crippled ones like matchsticks to whisk them back and forth between beds and chairs.

A badly-retarded girl named Josie lived in the Untidy Ward. Josie was about twelve years old, and though she could speak in simple phrases, she said very little, just walked around aimlessly or sat and stared the entire day. One morning as Della Raye started to change Josie's bed, she found crimson streaks of blood staining the sheets. She gingerly pulled the top sheet down and saw a small, bloody object lying in the middle of the bed. At first she couldn't identify the object, so she flipped the sheet to turn it over. Her eyes grew wide as she recognized the grisly thing—the distal joint of an index finger, crudely severed from a human hand.

"Miss Herman!" Della shouted in alarm.

Fanny Herman came running, stopped short, and pointed at the middle of Josie's bed. "My Lord! What's that?" the attendant asked.

"It's part of somebody's finger," Della answered.

"Oh my God!" Miss Herman said. "Where's Josie?"

They ran to the bathroom, and there they found Josie. Standing silent and alone, with bloodstains covering her nightgown, the girl was staring blankly at the bloody stump of her finger.

"What happened, Josie?!" Miss Herman asked. "What happened to your finger, honey?" Josie allowed the attendant to examine the jagged stump, but said nothing.

"Why, this looks like somebody bit it off!" Miss Herman said. "Josie, who did this to you?" The girl continued to stare at the bloody remnant of her finger but would tell them nothing of what had happened. And she never did.

We found out later who did it. It was another girl in the Untidy Ward. She sneaked down to Josie's bed in the middle of the night and bit her finger off, and Josie never made a sound.

Although Partlow existed primarily to house the feeble-minded, a few psychotics ended up there as well. One was a tall, wild-eyed woman named Rachel who lived in the Untidy Ward. Unlike most of the retarded patients around her, Rachel had no physical deformities; in fact, she was healthy and quite strong.

During storms the patients tended to become agitated and frightened, a reaction much like that of small children. During thunder and lightning displays many of them would huddle together like abandoned animals, while others lay on the floor in a fetal position, moaning and wailing in their fear.

Rachel reacted to storms differently. As the thunder reverberated across the hills and lightning lit up the tall windows, the deranged woman would stalk up and down the ward, her wild eyes rolling as if she were possessed, and shout in a voice that seemed only to encourage the angry elements, "BE NOT DISMAYED. WE ARE IN GOD'S HANDS." The words may have been spiritual in nature, but her protestations offered little comfort to the terrified patients. They huddled even closer together and looked at Rachel as if they had more to fear than just the storm.

Rachel watched Della Raye constantly, and glared at her with hatred. Della noticed that the attendants kept Rachel as far away from her as possible, and one day she asked Fanny Herman why. "That woman scares me, Miss Herman. Why does she keep looking at me like that?"

"Because Rachel hates blond curly hair like yours," the attendant explained.

"But she's got blond curly hair herself!" Della said incredulously.

"I know," Miss Herman replied, "but she's crazy. She used to live in the high-grade ward till her sister took her home for a visit. While she was watching her sister's baby, Rachel lit a burner on the stove and tried to set the baby on it. Her sister caught her just as she was about to burn the baby up, and brought her back to Partlow that minute. After that she really got crazy, and they put her here in the Untidy Ward."

"She's got mean eyes," Della exclaimed, "and she keeps watching me all the time."

"She'd kill you if she could," the attendant warned, "just because of those blond curls. Rachel's a lot bigger than you, Della Raye, and she's strong, and crazy as a loon. You watch out for her. She's dangerous."

W. D. Partlow visited the institution once a week on a regular basis. The director was usually escorted wherever he went by an entourage consisting of Dr. Woodruff and his supervisors, but one cold day as Della Raye was dressing to go outside, the famous man surprised her.

While pulling on her coat, Della had somehow lost track of her cap. Thinking herself alone in the ward, she was frantically turning down her sheet, lifting her pillow, and looking under her bed when she sensed another's presence. Turning around quickly, she discovered a tall, distinguished man watching her curiously.

With his strong features, prominent eyebrows, dark piercing eyes, and steel gray hair whitening at the edges, Dr. Partlow fit the role of director perfectly. Caught by surprise and overly excited, Della Raye blurted, "Oh, my Lord," then quickly covered her mouth in embarrassment.

A hint of amusement crossed the director's face. "What are you looking for, little lady?" he asked.

"I'm, uh, looking for my cap," Della stammered.

His eyes twinkled. "Well, you've got one on your head," he told her.

"Oh, my gosh!" Della said, reaching up to find the lost cap sitting atop her own head. "Thanks, Dr. Partlow," she said with a grin.

He smiled, nodded, and walked on.

He was just like that. I probably didn't see him but about once a month, but Dr. Partlow was always nice to us.

Sometime during her pre-teen years, Della Raye became interested in hair styling. She first began experimenting with her own, then moved on to her friends. Having no tools or materials with which to work, she used rolled-up snuff cans and pencils for curlers. And though she taught herself with these homemade devices, Della soon gained a reputation for her styling skill. The girls would vie for the opportunity to have her curl their hair, then strut around the ward proudly showing it off to the others. Although she had no way of knowing it at the time, in learning to style hair with those makeshift curlers, Della Raye sparked the beginnings of a life-long vocation.

At about the same time she gained another interest, one that would affect her life more than she could ever imagine. Della Raye had often noticed a clean-cut boy across the room at the dances and movies. He seemed easy going and displayed nicer manners than most of the others, and though she had never so much as stood close to him, his blond hair, blue eyes, and thin, kind face caught her attention. Della thought the boy had noticed her too.

"That's Homer Duncan," her friend Maryanne told her. "He's my boyfriend."

"Your boyfriend?!" Della answered. "How can he be your boyfriend?"

"'Cause me and Homer write notes back and forth to each other," Maryanne explained with obvious pride.

"Notes? How in the world do you get notes to each other?" Della asked.

"Can't tell you that," Maryanne said. "It's a secret."

Then one day a kindly middle-aged attendant named Bessie Waterman handed Della Raye a small piece of paper. "This is from Homer Duncan," she said under her breath. "Hide it, and don't tell anybody where you got it."

Stunned by the surprise note, as well as the clandestine involvement of Miss Waterman, Della Raye quickly pocketed the paper. Later that evening she unfolded it in private. "Dear A-1," the note began. "This is from A-2. If we use our real names we'll get in trouble. I seen you at the dances and the movies, and I sure do like you. I think you're real pretty too. Would you write me a note back?" The message ended with, "Love, A-2."

"Oh Lord!" she thought. Maryanne was one of her best friends, and Della had just received a love note from her boyfriend.

Bessie Waterman, the attendant who had handed her the note, was one of the few married employees. In a situation similar to that of the Samuels, both Bessie and her husband worked at Partlow and lived on the grounds. Mr. Waterman was a kindly, crippled attendant who worked in the Boys Ward where Homer lived. And now Della knew how the notes got passed—by way of the Watermans.

She sent a reply. "Dear A-2," Della wrote to Homer. "I liked getting your note, and I think you're nice too. But I thought you were Maryanne's boyfriend. What are you going to tell her about us? Write me and let me know. Sincerely, A-1."

Upon receiving her reply, Homer sent Maryanne a final note, explaining that he liked Della Raye more than he liked her. The unwelcome news caused a rift between Della and Maryanne that would last for some time, though they eventually made up. In the meantime, Homer and Della traded notes back and forth by way of the Watermans.

Having been committed to Partlow as a young child, Homer's life had paralleled Della Raye's. And they had more in common than just their backgrounds; he was obviously smarter than most of the boys there and possessed a high mechanical aptitude as well. Instead of sending him to work at the Boys Colony, Partlow capitalized on his abilities by making him an assistant to the head maintenance man.

Della Raye and Homer remained A-1 and A-2 in their secret notes, but they soon began calling each other "honey," "sweetheart," and other such endearments. They never had the opportunity to hold hands or to even speak with one another, but their treasured notes helped them span the chasm of loneliness that both knew too well. And their innocent, cryptic messages would spawn a relationship with farther-reaching effects than either of them could have guessed in those young years.

CHAPTER FIVE

The Terrible Teens

By the time she reached her teens, Della Raye had been a patient at Partlow for more than nine years, and still never classified as a moron, imbecile, or idiot. A physician's report at age eleven had read ". . . general appearance defective looking," and gone on to say: "She is doing third grade work in school and gets along nicely with the other children."

Records indicate that Dr. Woodruff tested Della's IQ a second time when she was thirteen. This time her IQ calculated 61 as opposed to her previous score of 67. Interestingly, a handwritten note on the test sheet (jotted there by Dr. Woodruff?), stated that she "Could have done better." And again, had her true age been used in the calculation she would have tested normal.

As Della Raye was undressing to take a shower one day, the sight of bloodstains in her underwear startled her. When she saw blood flowing down the shower drain, her concern turned to fright. "I've got cancer," she thought. "I've got cancer and I'm going to die."

She was too afraid to tell anyone of her suspected cancer. That night she lay awake praying that she would live, and checking continually to see if the bleeding had stopped.

After a few days she found that the blood flow had increased. Della went into the bathroom alone and filled the tub. Trying desperately to wash away the blood, she undressed and sat down in the water. The bleeding wouldn't stop. As the bath water began to cloud red, Maryanne came through the door.

"What are you doing in the tub, Della Raye?" Maryanne asked. Della was too afraid to answer.

Maryanne's eyes grew wide as she approached the tub. "What's wrong, Della Raye? You're bleeding!"

"I know," Della said. "I've been bleeding for several days. I think I've got cancer, Maryanne. I think I'm going to die."

"You haven't told anybody about this?" Maryanne asked.

"No, I've been afraid to."

"I'll be right back," the girl said, and ran out the door.

In less than a minute Mama Leonard came charging through the door, Maryanne following close behind. "What's wrong, Della Raye?" the big woman asked with concern.

"I'm afraid I've got cancer, Mama Leonard," Della answered in a quavering voice. "I think I'm dying."

Mama Leonard looked at the bath water and quickly assessed the situation. Her eyes went from concern to relief, then to understanding. "Oh honey," she said with a reassuring grin. "You haven't got cancer. It's just something that happens to girls when they get your age. You're going to be all right."

Della Raye nearly cried with relief. "Come on, get out and dry off," Mama Leonard said. The kind woman then sat down and explained the menstrual cycle to her and taught her how to deal with it.

Della Raye had lived in the Main Building since the age of four. The Number Two Building housed the low-functioning male patients, and a few high-grades like Homer, while a smaller structure served as the female Untidy Building. A new dormitory went up at the Boys Colony in the mid-1930s, and a few years later, another was added at Partlow—the Number Three Building. These were the buildings that W. D. Partlow funded by raising cash crops at the Colony.

Della Raye moved to the new dormitory in her early teens. The Number Three Building may have been new, but the ward was colorless, crowded, and every bit as depressing as the old one. Attendant living quarters occupied one wing of the ground floor, so now the female attendants lived just across the rotunda from Della.

Lula, Maryanne, Grace, Mary, and several other girls she had known most of her life moved to the new building with her, and now that they were older, they shared the ward with adult patients. Lorita Fricard's flamboyance provided comic relief, but she was far from the oddest patient in the ward.

Essie, a freakish woman whom Della had often seen in the yard and the dining room, lived in her ward. Essie was tall and stoutly built, a deformed giant with six fingers on each hand and a horribly wide face with big, protruding eyes that threatened to pop out of their sockets. And now that Della Raye lived with Essie and showered with her, she discovered even more bizarre features. Along with the extra fingers the gargantuan woman also had six toes on each foot and two sets of breasts. One could see that Essie's breasts were large and saggy under a dress, but Della hadn't known about the extra pair. In the shower, the woman would pick up one of her big, sack-like breasts and throw it over her shoulder, where it would stay on its own, revealing a smaller, poorly-developed one beneath. She would then wash the smaller breast, flop the larger one back in place, and throw the other one over the opposite shoulder to repeat the process.

Essie's large, protruding eyes gave her a wild, demonic look. Coupled with the enormity of her body and its outlandish deformities, this bug-eyed glare made the woman look deranged and fearsome. An unfortunate quirk of nature, for Essie was simply a decent person trapped in a freak's body.

The woman didn't look like a human being. She looked like some sort of giant or something, but she wasn't mean at all. She was friendly, and just as nice as she could be. Her mind was all right too. I suppose somebody put her in there because they were ashamed of her.

As her reputation for hair styling continued to grow, Della Raye had to find more innovative ways to make curlers. Patients would bring her various objects such as pencils and empty lipstick tubes and ask her to please, "Do my hair." Often she had time to do only half of a patient's head in the morning and then finish it in the evening. When that happened, the woman would have to walk around all day with one side of her hair curled and the other side hanging straight down, but Della's simple customers didn't seem to mind. When she finished, like beaming children, they would primp, strut, and show off their new hairdos.

One memorable day Della Raye heard a soft "Hello" behind her. She turned and looked into a face that would change her life forever. Delia Matthews—a quiet, serene attendant with dark, knowing eyes and fine, wavy hair, framing smoothly rounded cheeks of silken olive skin—was a beautiful lady inside and out.

The new attendant quickly gained such popularity among the girls that they christened her with their own endearing name. Addressing her as Miss Matthews sounded too formal and impersonal, and since they were forbidden to use her given name, she became "Massie." And though the use of such a nickname was against regulations, even the other attendants soon began calling her Massie. Considerate, soft-spoken and sure, Massie possessed a rare mixture of tenderness and compassion coupled with strength and integrity—a miracle combination for an attendant.

Massie's old-school honesty would not allow her even to tell a white lie, but because everyday medicines such as aspirins and laxatives were not made available to the patients, she spent part of her meager wage buying medications for the girls and risked her job dispensing them. And she spent a bit more on chewing gum and special treats for Della Raye.

Della must have loved Massie instantly; she can't remember not loving her. And though she hovered at Massie's side constantly, the quiet lady never complained; even Della's incessant talking didn't seem to bother her. For the first time in her life, Della felt totally secure with an adult, free from the confines of holding her feelings in check as she had conditioned herself to do.

One evening as Massie's shift was ending, she touched Della Raye on the shoulder and said, "Good night, Della. I'll see you in the morning."

Della's response was something that a patient never ever did to an attendant. She wrapped her arms around Massie's shoulders, hugged her and said, "I love you, Massie."

Briefly, but without hesitation, Massie returned the hug. "I love you too, Della Raye," she replied, turned and walked quickly out the door.

I even felt jealous when Massie did something for the other girls. She was my Mama.

Christmas at Partlow was hopelessly meager. In later years public donations provided presents for the children, but during the Depression, few had anything to give. Each girl was allowed to order a single gift a few days before Christmas; ten cents was the maximum she could spend. On Christmas day their gifts appeared at the Schoolhouse under a tree decorated with glass bulbs and paper cutouts colored with crayons.

Oscar Samuel, the tall, lanky husband of the supervisor Madelyn, and her opposite in temperament, delighted in helping the girls with their gifts. He and the women attendants would pass out the packages and help the badly retarded girls unwrap theirs. A bit of candy, a ball, or a little book made their holiday.

Della Raye always spent her ten cents on a gift for Massie. One year she had ordered a box of handkerchiefs, but when she unwrapped the box on Christmas day she found it empty. "Mr. Samuel," she cried. "All I got was an empty box!"

The man hurried across the room. "What was supposed to be in it, Della Raye?" Mr. Samuel asked with concern.

"Handkerchiefs," she said, nearly in tears. "I was going to give them to Massie for her Christmas present."

He stood thinking for a moment, then said, "Give me that box, Della Raye." She handed it to him and he hurried out the door.

She never learned where Mr. Samuel went with the box,

but a few minutes later, he walked back in with a smile on his face and handed it to her. Della Raye opened it and found it filled with new white handkerchiefs. "Thanks so much, Mr. Samuel," she said with relief. "It's the only thing I get to do for her."

Another caring lady came to work as a night attendant. Anna Lee Dockery was young, petite, and pretty. And unlike Massie, who had become Della's mother figure, Miss Dockery seemed more like an older sister. Though it flew in the face of regulations, she would come through the ward after lights out, wake up Della, and take her to the rotunda, where they would sit on the stairs and tell stories and laugh and giggle far into the night.

While walking in the yard one day, Della wandered near the edge where the ground sloped steeply down toward the exposed roots of a large oak. Feeling frisky and more than a little mischievous, she glanced around to see if any attendants were watching. Finding no one looking her direction, Della casually sauntered back to the center of the yard, whirled, and ran toward the oak as fast as she could go. Halfway down the slope, she turned sideways and dove for the ground with outstretched arms. She planned to do a tremendous cartwheel, but the slope fooled her. As her feet turned in a wide arc above her head, her hands slipped beneath her and she crashed, headfirst, into a heavy root protruding from the ground.

Rolling into a crumpled heap beneath the tree, Della Raye grabbed her splitting head and looked back up the slope into the yard. No one had seen her. She quickly jumped up and brushed the dirt and leaves from her hair and saw blood on her hands. The back of her head was bleeding. She tried to wipe it away, but the more she wiped the more it bled.

Knowing she'd be in trouble if anyone discovered what she had done, Della ran back up the hill directly at an attendant and pretended to trip and fall on the back of her head next to the woman. She grabbed her bleeding head, picked herself up off the ground, and asked permission to go inside and get her cap. She stuffed rags inside her cap to stop the bleeding, but the idea didn't work; the rags only acted as a sponge.

That night when she heard the attendant's footsteps approaching down the center aisle, she called out quietly in the dark, "Miss Dockery, can you help me?"

"What's wrong, Della?" the young woman whispered.

"I'm bleeding," she said, "and I can't get it to stop."

"Bleeding!" Miss Dockery exclaimed. "Come with me, Della."

Della Raye followed her into the rotunda. "Where are you bleeding?" she asked. Della pointed at the back of her head. Miss Dockery parted her hair and said, "Oh Lord. You wait here while I go get the first-aid kit."

When she returned, Miss Dockery sat Della down on the stairs and began to clean and dress the wound. "How in the world did this happen, girl?" she asked.

Della hesitated, then told her. "I was out in the yard today and tried to turn a cartwheel down off that steep bank."

"A cartwheel?!"

"Yes. I didn't make it, though. I fell and hit my head on a big tree root. Nobody saw me do it, but I couldn't get the bleeding to stop."

"Whatever made you want to turn a cartwheel?"

"I was just trying to have some fun," Della said.

Miss Dockery sighed and shook her head. "Oh, Della Raye. I'd help you escape from here if I could."

Along with her regular attendant's job, Massie was in charge of the marking room. In order to avoid clothing getting mixed up at the laundry, every item worn by patients had to be marked with the owner's name. Massie spent some of her afternoons marking clothes and worked many evenings as well.

Della Raye often volunteered to help Massie in the evening. Marking hundreds of items of clothing while separating and shifting them from one stack to another was hard work; but that way she got to spend a few hours with Massie. The dresses they marked were mostly white, though occasionally a flowered one came through that had been made from colored flour sacks saved by the kitchen employees.

The marking room was located on the second floor of the Main Building. Hidden away in a remote corner, it usually provided Massie and Della Raye complete privacy to talk while they worked. This consisted mostly of Della talking and Massie listening, of course.

One evening before they began work, Massie smiled at Della and said, "I've got something for you."

"Something for me?" Della said excitedly, and Massie handed her a large box. Della looked at it with wonder, too shocked to move.

"Go ahead, open it up," Massie said, the hint of a twinkle in her soft eyes. Della Raye opened the box, grew wide-eyed, and gasped. It was a new dress, handmade, with scores of beautiful flowers dancing over its billowy surface. Massie had saved her own flour sacks at home, cut out the pattern herself, and stitched it by hand. Della Raye looked closely at the stitches. They were tiny, and every seam was backstitched with care, the finest and most painstaking way to handsew a garment.

The tiny stitches reminded Della Raye of her favorite childhood story, a book titled Freckles. The main character in Freckles was an orphan boy whose mother had died when he was a baby. The circumstances surrounding his mother's death had left him wondering all his life if she had loved him. Then his girlfriend found his long-lost baby clothes, showed them to him, and pointed at the stitches. "I never in all my life saw such dainty, fine little stitches," the orphan's girlfriend said. "And as for loving you, no boy's mother ever loved you more!"

I thought about that story when I saw the dress. Massie had back-stitched every seam in it, with love.

Della stood looking at the dress, unable to speak. Finally Massie grinned and said, "Well, put it on Della Raye. Let's see how it looks."

Della removed her drab institutional dress, lay it aside, and carefully slipped on the new one. It fit perfectly. Looking down the front of the dress, she beamed at the happy flowers and marveled at their dancing colors. "Oh, Massie. I've never seen anything so beautiful," she said.

Massie sat grinning widely as Della whirled around, showing off her new dress. Suddenly, a figure darkened the doorway. Madelyn Samuel surveyed the scene coldly. "What's going on here?" the supervisor asked. "What are you doing with a dress like that, Della Raye?" she said, eyeing it narrowly.

Della looked at her blankly and said nothing. The woman's eyes blazed. "Where did you get it?!" she demanded. Della refused to answer.

Without looking at Massie or acknowledging her presence, Miss Samuel continued to press Della Raye. "You stole those flour sacks from the kitchen, didn't you?" Della remained silent. "Uh huh, I figured that's where you got them," the woman said with venom in her voice.

A pair of scissors lay within Miss Samuel's reach. She picked them up, bent down to the hem of Della's new dress, snipped it through, and quickly ran the scissors upward, splitting the front open from hem to neck. Then grabbing one side of the split dress in each hand, in a single motion, she ripped it off Della's body.

The supervisor wadded the tattered remains of the dress into the crook of her arm and coolly marched away. Massie sat limply in her chair, tears rolling down her cheeks. "Why didn't you tell her where you got the dress, Della Raye?" she asked.

"I couldn't tell her, Massie," Della answered. "I knew you'd lose your job if I did."

Della Raye sank to the floor. They cried, for a long, long time.

Massie bought Della some real curlers, and with those her hair styling became quite professional. Now the attendants decided to take advantage of her skills. Since they lived just across the rotunda from her, the attendants would bring Della Raye to their quarters in the evening and make her do their hair, often several at a time. Sometimes they made jokes about paying her, but none of them ever did. They were just saving the expense of having it done in town. One of the attendants did give her a dress in appreciation for her work, a hand-me-down rag so threadbare that Della was ashamed to wear it, even in the institution.

Another form of exploitation began taking place among the teenage girls. Young medical students started coming to Partlow to practice physical examinations. The exams seemed harmless at first—listen to the heart, look at the teeth, measure blood pressure, etc. Then Della Raye heard some of the girls complaining of more intimate procedures. The students were making them strip, so they could look at their breasts and perform invasive genital probing.

The exams took place in a small room set up especially for the purpose, and for some reason Massie always had to sit in the room and observe them. Massie hated watching the girls undergo such humiliation, but she said nothing in protest. Possibly, she had been selected as an observer because of her passiveness.

One morning Della Raye learned that she was on the list of girls to be examined that day. Several young men watched her intently as she entered the room later that afternoon. Massie sat in a chair off to one side, her eyes pained to see Della subjected to such degradation.

"Go ahead, young lady," one of the men said. "Take all your clothes off."

Della Raye slipped off her dress but did not remove her bra. Then she bent down, pulled off her panties and straightened back up, revealing a sanitary napkin covering her private parts. She gazed at the students innocently as they exchanged quizzical glances. Marveling at Della's cunning, Massie sat pokerfaced. She knew Della had worn the napkin simply to discourage them.

The young men looked at each other a few moments, shrugged, and turned back to Della. The one who had told her to undress spoke again. "Put your clothes back on," he said, disgusted. "We'll take the next girl."

Della slipped her dress on and started for the door, catching Massie's eyes on the way out. A furtive glance passed between them, and she was gone.

Those students were just using the girls for guinea pigs, humiliating them something awful. But not a one of them ever saw me or touched me that way.

Ultimately, an attendant went to Millie Hennessy and reported what the medical students were doing. The supervisor immediately put a stop to the exams. Della Raye never learned if it was Massie who finally turned them in.

Homer's notes to Della Raye often ended with, "I love you, A-2." She felt honored to think that someone might care for her so deeply, but though she continued to call him sweetheart and looked forward to seeing his handsome smile across the room at the movies and dances, Della never felt inclined to return Homer's professions of love.

Homer continued writing notes to Della Raye and never failed to sign them: "Love, A-2." She always replied, but never with the same degree of affection that he expressed. One day she received a message that said, "I might be getting out pretty soon. I'd like that, but I'll miss you something awful if I'm gone."

Della wrote back, "Dear A-2, I'd miss you too, but that would be wonderful if you could get out. I pray every night to get out of here but I don't see how it could ever happen. Sincerely, A-1."

A few days later, Bessie Waterman handed Della the last note she would ever receive from Homer. "Dear A-1," it began. "It's true. I am going to get out, and soon. Seems like I've been in here forever. I'm going to miss you, though. I love you more than anybody in the world, and someday I'm going to get you out of here too. Love, A-2."

She would miss his notes and his warm smile at the dances and movies, but she was happy for him. They had never touched nor exchanged a single word, but Della Raye felt that Homer was one of the finest people she would ever meet.

Work became a more serious matter as Della grew into her teens. She and Maryanne worked in the linen room, stacking sheets and pillowcases on the shelves. Being small and agile, Maryanne worked on the tall ladder while Della handed her the linens.

Della Raye got involved in an argument with a retarded woman one morning, but walked away and tried to let the matter drop. Later that day, the woman walked into the linen room, looked at Della, and immediately grew angry again. Della tried to calm her down, while Maryanne waited on the ladder above them.

"Go on now," Della told the simple woman. "I don't want any trouble with you." But the woman grew madder and finally threw a punch. Della returned the blow, and the fight was on.

Her lumbering adversary was poorly coordinated but feisty and strong, and despite her clumsiness, she put up a worthy fight. Suddenly, as the two dodged and parried, something heavy whacked the top of the woman's head. To Della's dismay, her opponent's arms dropped; her face went blank; and she walked stiffly out the door, without so much as looking up to see what had hit her.

Della looked up and saw a grinning Maryanne standing on the ladder. "Sure glad somebody left that old shoe up here," she said, laughing as she spoke.

"Yeah, me too," Della answered. They laughed out loud, then returned to their work.

When the linen room job ended, she went to work full-time in the ironing room. Della's manual dexterity made ironing easy, but the room arrangement created a problem. It consisted of two parallel lines of ironing boards, with a long narrow space between them. Facing one another across the space, the girls stood on the outside of each line as they ironed. The boards were fastened securely to the floor and positioned to accommodate right-handed ironers only. Della Raye was left-handed. In order to iron, she had to stand on the opposite side of her board. This placed her in the space between the boards, her rear end facing the opposite line of girls.

The temptation was too great. Every few minutes one of the girls would reach over and tap Della's behind with the tip of her steaming iron. They would all squeal with delight as she grabbed her rear end and ran to the other side of her board.

It was funny, but I got tired of them running me over to the other side so I had to learn to iron right handed.

At age fourteen came the job Della would hate—the kitchen. She first worked in the bakery, along with ten other patients, then graduated to the kitchen, which employed about twenty-five. Her day began at 4:00 A.M. and didn't end until the supper dishes had been washed, dried, and put away in the evening.

Her mother worked in the kitchen too, and though Della would sometimes see Ruby glancing at her from across the room, they didn't speak. Then one day their eyes met and lingered a moment. The next time it happened, Della said, "Hello, Mama."

Ruby's simple face lit up. With hopeful eyes and a tentative smile, she replied, "Hi, Della Raye." A small exchange, but a moment that served as the beginning of a long, long healing.

Della's height remained average at fourteen, but her body had filled out, and she had lost her skinniness. She had strength and stamina, and though she hated the kitchen, she worked hard and did her best to stay out of trouble. At that age she felt more rebellious than ever, but she fought to control it.

Betty Myers was badly addicted to snuff and, like Della's Aunt Dovie, she grew more irritable when her supply was running low. When the kitchen supervisor hollered, "Della Raye, you get your ass to movin'!" she would bite her tongue and resist replying. The crazy Mona McCurty didn't bother Della Raye at all, and to her surprise, the sloppy Myra Helpman didn't either. Della was aware that Myra mistreated the feebleminded workers, and one day she asked her mother about it.

"Aw, Myra don't treat nobody too bad," Ruby said. But when Della pressed her, her mother looked at the floor and said, "Well, when any of us has lipstick or anything like that she takes it away from us, and she never does give it back."

Della watched Myra closely after that, and eyed her with obvious mistrust. The woman must have gotten the message; she never bothered Ruby again as long as Della worked in the kitchen.

From morning till night Della Raye lifted hundred-pound sacks of flour and potatoes, carried armloads of heavy pots and pans, washed thousands of dishes, and stirred huge cauldrons of food with a paddle the size of a boat oar. But even in that sweaty kitchen she looked for fun wherever she could find it. Sometimes, though—like the cartwheel incident—her best efforts didn't work out.

Della Raye was trying to lighten things up in the kitchen one day, oddly enough, while washing dishes. Working alone, she was scrubbing tin plates and silverware, when she began to sing. Keeping time with her singing, she started tossing plates, knives, forks, and spoons from the soapy dishwater into the pan of rinse water. The rhythm picked up speed until Della was dancing wildly back and forth, singing loudly, and slinging utensils vigorously into the splashing water. Caught up in her own reverie and racket, she didn't hear Millie Hennessy walk up behind her.

"What in the world's going on here?!" Miss Hennessy shouted, and grabbed Della Raye by the shoulder. Startled at the sudden intrusion, Della Raye whirled around and swung wildly. Miss Hennessy caught a solid blow to the chest and reeled backward on her crippled legs. She lost her balance and went down hard on her back, smacking her head against a large metal pot as she fell.

Before Della could even realize what she had done, the

fallen supervisor grabbed her head and cried, "He-elp!" Several employees stormed toward them as Miss Hennessy lay on her back, waving her arms wildly and screaming: "Take her to the Cross Hall! Take her to the Cross Hall!"

The attendants grabbed Della roughly and half-carried, half-dragged her from the kitchen to the Untidy Building. There, they propelled her down the hallway that reeked of human stench, threw her into a dark hole, and slammed the barred door behind her. Della sank heavily to the floor, scooted onto the dirty pallet, and stared into the gloom.

Sitting in the semi-darkness the next morning, Della Raye heard the approach of a familiar, limping step. Looking up, she saw Miss Hennessy peering through the wooden bars. "Good morning, Della," the supervisor said. "How are you doing?" Della didn't answer. "I'm sorry I told them to put you in here," Miss Hennessy said. "It all just happened so sudden."

"I know," Della Raye answered. "I didn't mean to hit you, Miss Hennessy. You just caught me by surprise and I started swinging."

"Hang on, Della," she said. "I don't think you'll be in there very long."

Later that afternoon, Dr. Woodruff came by. She couldn't remember ever talking to him, except for when he gave her those stupid tests. "Hello, Della Raye," he said through the bars. She didn't answer. "Miss Hennessy tells me she thinks you didn't really mean to hit her, Della Raye. What have you got to say about that?"

Della looked at the floor for a moment, then spoke. "No, sir, I didn't mean to. She walked up behind me and startled me, and I just automatically turned around and hit her."

"Well, Della Raye," he said, "you shouldn't be so quick to hit somebody, certainly not a supervisor!"

"I know I shouldn't," Della answered. "She just caught me by surprise."

Dr. Woodruff warmed to his work. "Miss Hennessy said you were singing and carrying on while you were working in the kitchen too, Della Raye. That's no way to do your job. We've all got jobs to do here, and she doesn't have time to see that you do yours correctly every minute, let alone put up with violence. This is a big, big place, Della Raye, and I'm trying to make it as good as I can for you, but you've got to pitch in and do your part too."

"I know," she sighed, knowing she had not yet heard all of the lecture.

Della was released the following morning. She went to her ward to take a shower, then back to the kitchen to work. When she returned late that evening, she saw Mama Herman perched in a chair beside the bathroom door. The door was standing open, but Mama Herman was up to her old tricks. Sitting with her massive arms folded across her chest, she had propped her thick legs up on the seat of a second chair to block the doorway.

Della shed her soiled work clothes, gathered up her toiletries, and headed for the shower. At the bathroom door, she stopped and silently confronted Mama Herman. The big woman looked at her with a cool grin and said, "Bathroom's closed. Ain't nobody gonna bathe tonight."

Della Raye looked her in the eye and said coldly, "I've been working in that sweaty kitchen all day long, and I'm going in there and take a shower." With that, she stepped over the woman's legs and proceeded into the bathroom. Mama Herman remained seated, and said no more.

That was the only run-in I ever had with Mama Herman. She was a terrible bully, but for some reason she never seemed to mess with me very much.

Some patients didn't escape Mama Herman's wrath so easily. A retarded girl named Mattie needed to use the bathroom one evening when the bully woman had it blocked.

When Mattie had to urinate, the simple girl had a strange way of announcing it. Using a bit of backwoods slang she had learned before coming to Partlow, she would say: "Mattie has to make a branch." So while Mama Herman stood with her huge frame covering the bathroom door, the girl walked up to her and said, "Mattie has to make a branch."

"Not now, Mattie," Mama Herman told her. "Bathroom's closed."

"But Mattie needs to make a branch," she persisted.

Mama Herman exploded. "I said not now! Get outta here, Mattie. You'll just have to wait awhile."

Mattie walked away, but after only a few minutes she returned. Stopping again in front of Mama Herman, she looked up at her and pleaded, "Mattie has to make a branch." The giant woman reached out and grabbed two huge handfuls of Mattie's hair. Lifting the girl off the floor easily, Mama Herman began to swing Mattie, by her hair, in a circle. Around and around, faster and faster, she swung the helpless girl, glee lighting her devil's eyes. Mattie's body stood nearly straight out as she whirled.

Mattie never uttered a sound. Finally, Mama Herman stopped spinning her, and holding the girl at eye level, like a ragdoll, let go of her hair and dropped her to the floor on her feet.

"There now, how'd that feel?" she asked with a self-satisfied grin.

"Well, that didn't feel too good, Mama Herman," Mattie replied. "But I've still got to go to the bathroom."

Della stayed out of trouble for a while, then one day Betty Myers hollered at her mother. "Ruby Rogers, get yerself out there in the storehouse and bring me a hundred-pound sack of sugar."

As Ruby turned and trudged out the door, Myers shook her head impatiently and started after her. As she rounded the corner, she shouted back over her shoulder, "Della Rogers, you come out here and help her."

Myers was standing directly behind Ruby when Della Raye caught up to them. As Ruby started to bend over to pick up the sugar, Myers yelled, "Pick up that sugar! Bend that damn back!" She drew back her foot and kicked Ruby hard in the rear.

Della Raye exploded. She leaped onto the woman's back, grabbed her around the neck with one hand, and began pounding her with the other. Ruby looked around in horror as Della, beating her in the head viciously, clung to the wiry woman's back like a wild animal. Myers swung her body around furiously, trying to throw Della off. "Help!" she screamed, and again several employees came running to the rescue.

"Take her to the Cross Hall!" Myers yelled as the attendants tore Della Raye off her back. "Throw her ass in there and keep her for all I care."

Again Della was dragged to the Cross Hall and thrown into a dark cell. As the heavy door slammed shut, an attendant peered through the bars and sneered, "You done it this time, girl."

Later that evening, as Della sat on her pallet, leaning against the wall in the dark, the door flew open; and a second pallet was thrown against the opposite wall. "You've got company, Della Raye," an attendant's mocking voice announced.

She looked up to see the figure of a tall, stout woman silhouetted in the doorway, on her head the unmistakable outline of curly hair. A squinting look at the shadowy face revealed a dark, leering grin. Della rose to her feet warily. Her chest tightened as the woman stepped into the cell, the hungry gleam in the psychotic eyes penetrating the tight space between them.

"Rachel's going to be your roommate tonight, Della Raye," the attendant said with sadistic glee. At that, the lock turned in the door and the attendant's footsteps disappeared down the hall.

Trapped in the tiny cell, Della Raye felt sure she heard the pounding of her own heart echoing off the walls. Choking back the terror rising in her throat, she turned on Rachel like a cornered animal. To her shocked surprise, the crazy woman sat down on her pallet. Della stood tensely on her feet for several minutes, then sat down on hers. With scarcely a sound, the woman lay down and stretched out. Certain that Rachel was facing her, but barely able to see in the near darkness, Della couldn't tell if the woman's eyes were open or closed.

Della Raye lay down too. Facing Rachel, she scooted her back against the wall and determined not to close her eyes for even a moment. Squinting to see as best as she could, she watched the still figure closely. A lunatic—a kill-crazy woman who had stalked her daily in the Untidy Ward—lay two feet away. Della Raye was strong for her age, but her age was fourteen.

She lay, praying silently, for what seemed an eternity. Sometime after midnight, she heard Rachel begin to move and watched her rise to a sitting position. Slowly, Rachel turned her head toward Della and stealthily stood up. A cat stalking its prey on silent feet, Rachel stepped close.

Della Raye listened to the woman's heavy breathing, choked back a scream, and lay frozen at her feet. From the moment Rachel entered the cell, she had feared she might die. As the psycho stood over her panting with excitement, she thought the time had come.

Suddenly, Della's body tensed like a coiled spring, and something inside her said "No." Her survivor's soul could not abide this—her life would not end in a stinking dungeon at the hands of a maniac.

With a savage leap Della Raye was on her feet, her face thrust into Rachel's. "Damn you, Rachel!" she screamed. "I'll kill you! You lay a finger on me and I'll kill you with my bare hands! I swear I will!"

A skulking serpent caught in mid-stalk, Rachel froze. Eye-to-eye, they stood motionless for long minutes; then slowly the feral gleam in the crazy woman's eyes began to dim. She turned, dropped to her pallet, and lay down.

Della Raye sensed a movement to the side, glanced toward the light, and saw the night nurse watching them through the narrow bars. When their eyes met, the nurse walked away.

Della lay down again, but not to sleep.

Rachel left the next morning, but Della Raye would spend another week in the Cross Hall.

Prior to the incidents with Millie Hennessy and Betty Myers that landed her in the Cross Hall, Della Raye's health report had said: "general appearance good, well nourished . . . has been in the best of health during the past year, and gets along nicely."

A report following the fight with Betty Myers was less complimentary. "This child has been working in the kitchen but on account of being so impudent and ugly talking it was necessary to send her to Ward E (the Cross Hall) for a short stay. She is a behavior problem, has an ugly disposition, and talks very disrespectful to those over her. Other than this she gets along very well and is enjoying good health."

Her next report, dated June 20, 1940, began with "Imbecile," a term reserved for the significantly retarded, patients with an IQ less than 55. Interestingly, on an IQ test taken just twelve days prior to this report, Della Raye had scored 67. And like the other test scores in her record, this one had been calculated incorrectly and artificially lowered.

Apparently, it didn't matter that Della Raye had completed the institutional school with ease, taught herself to read, absorbed every book in the library, and mastered every task given her. She was a troublemaker; and by the stroke of a pen, she was branded an imbecile.

When an employee who had access to patient records informed Massie that Della Raye had been diagnosed as an imbecile, Massie passed it on to Della. Della cared little about that; however, she didn't know what an imbecile was anyway. And when Massie gave her another stern lecture about staying out of trouble, Della replied, "But that woman kicked my own mother right in front of me. Am I supposed to just stand there and watch something like that and do nothing?"

"Most people in here would, Della Raye," Massie told her, "rather than go to the Cross Hall."

"Not me," Della said emphatically. "They can't treat people like that. It's just not right."

Massie shook her head and Lula prayed for her.

The only news of the outside world came from a radio that the attendants sometimes played in the ward. Most of the patients didn't listen to it; they didn't care about the news or understand it anyway.

Della Raye was sixteen when the United States entered World War II, but why should she be concerned about a war going on in a world that she knew little of? After all, she knew the names of only a few people outside the gates of Partlow: her Uncle Richard, Homer, and a few girls who had been released. She had lost contact with the girls; she had little memory of her uncle, a man she despised; and she never thought about Homer. She had long since forgotten Homer, as well as his promise to get her out of Partlow; and she had no way of knowing that he'd been called into the military and shipped overseas to fight.

At sixteen Della Raye was still working in the kitchen, still hating it, and concerning herself with more immediate things than a war and a childhood boyfriend she hadn't seen for years. At an age when a girl's life is blossoming, when she should have been spending her time laughing, dreaming, and sharing secrets with friends, trying to figure out which boy really was the best looking in school, and why one boy flirted with her constantly while another less attentive one seemed to rivet her attention, Della Raye spent her days working at slave labor and trying to stay out of trouble with Betty Myers.

Rena Scott left Partlow while Della was working in the kitchen. Though Della knew she would miss her former school teacher, Rena left her with a spark of hope that became an obsession. "Della Raye, keep your chin up and stay out of trouble," Rena said as she was leaving, "and I'm going to try and get you out of here as soon as I can."

Rena Scott's promise dominated Della's mind, but the hope it instilled in her ultimately led to her downfall.

Della Raye prayed for her freedom more than ever now; and the desire grew even stronger when five girls escaped, her friend Maryanne among them. The girls all worked in the laundry, where they had befriended a one-armed man who delivered coal to the boiler room in the same building. Like Maryanne, most of them were smart, and somehow they talked the man into sneaking them off the grounds in his coal truck.

The Partlow officials never figured out how the girls managed to escape, but Della Raye and her friends knew. A few nights after the incident, Lula was leading several of them in prayer. "Dear God," Lula said. "Thank you for helping our sisters get away. And wherever they are tonight, watch over them and keep them safe."

A retarded girl who worked in the laundry interrupted Lula's prayer to explain something. "Lula, it wasn't God helped them girls escape," she said. "It was that old one-armed man helped them get away."

"I know," Lula answered with a grin. "Just don't say that to anybody else."

Maryanne and the other four made good their escape; none of them were ever found. Knowing that the girls had gotten away, and obsessed with Rena Scott's promise, Della Raye dreamed of freedom constantly.

Having heard nothing from Rena after four months, Della grew despondent. Being impatient by nature, she began to think of escaping herself. She and a friend named Verna, who worked with her in the kitchen, often spoke of what they would do if they were free. One day Verna whispered to her, "I know how I could get a set of keys that would let us out of this place."

"Keys! How are you going to do that?" Della asked. "You know they keep them all over there in the Main Building. Every attendant gets handed a ring of keys when she comes on duty and then has to turn them back in when she gets off."

"I know," Verna answered. "Don't worry about how I'm going to do it, but I'll get the keys when we need them. And my sister's going with us when we go."

Verna's sister lived in another ward, so their escape plan would have to provide a way for the three of them to leave together. Because the girls would need someone on the outside to help them after they escaped the grounds, they decided to ask Shawna Fitzsimmons, a young attendant who showed a great amount of compassion for the patients. Shawna's sister, Elsie, who also worked at Partlow, lived in a house just across the street from the main gate.

Shawna Fitzsimmons happened to be dating a doctor from a nearby town, and enlisted his help. The attendant told the girls that she would arrange to be off the night they escaped, and that she and the doctor would meet them at her sister's house and spirit them away from Tuscaloosa in his car.

And so the plan was set. As promised, one Sunday evening Verna showed Della Raye a set of keys. "They won't be missed till tomorrow morning," Verna told her.

Shawna Fitzsimmons had recruited another attendant to bring Verna's sister to their ward after lights out. The three of them would unlock the door, walk out, and scale the fence. They would then meet Shawna and her doctor boyfriend at Elsie's house and leave the area.

Their plan developed a hitch. A girl in their ward noticed Della Raye and Verna whispering late that evening and guessed that they had something planned. When the girl confronted them, they admitted their plan to escape that night. "Unless you promise to take me with you, I'll turn you in," the girl told them. And though neither Della Raye nor Verna had confidence in her, they reluctantly told the girl she could come. "Okay," the girl said. "I'm gonna stay awake tonight, and you'd better not try to leave without me." They knew they had no choice.

The plan still seemed sound enough, but something else went awry. Della Raye and Verna waited and waited that night, but Verna's sister never came. They whispered about what might have gone wrong and wondered what they should do. Had they been found out? Had the keys already been missed? Was someone just waiting for them to make a move? And there was that other girl lying awake down there who insisted on leaving with them.

Lost in all the wondering and indecision, Della Raye and Verna never left the ward. Early the next morning, the keys were missed. No one knew who had them; but a crowd of locksmiths, which may have comprised every locksmith in Tuscaloosa, descended on Partlow and changed the locks on the inside and outside doors of every dormitory.

The Partlow officials concerned themselves with the security of the dormitories and wards but neglected to change the locks on the kitchen and main dining room. While Della Raye and Verna were working in the kitchen late that afternoon, they met in the empty dining room to discuss their situation.

"I've still got the keys in my pocket," Verna said, "and we're going to get in trouble over them one way or another."

Della Raye agreed. "You're right," she said. "If we're going to be in trouble anyway, why don't we just go?"

"Yeah, why not?"

They took off their aprons, unlocked the dining room door, and locked it behind them. As was often the case during the day, the main gate was standing open. Della Raye and Verna made it to the fence unseen, slipped along in the shadows of the overhanging trees, and walked out the gate. Having nowhere else to go, they crossed the street to Elsie's house, where they had been expected the night before.

"Where have you girls been?!" Elsie exclaimed. "Shawna and the doctor waited all night long for you." The girls explained what had happened and why they had not been able to leave. "What are you doing here now?" Elsie asked in exasperation. "It's too late."

"We know," Della said. "We figured we'd get in trouble over the keys anyway, so we just took off."

"They'll come here looking for you," Elsie told them. "They come to every house around here whenever somebody escapes, and I can't lie to them. If I do that, I'll lose my job."

"We know you can't," Della replied, resigned to her fate.

Within thirty minutes, two men came to the door. Della recognized them as Partlow employees. When the men asked

Elsie if she had seen two runaways, the attendant pointed into her living room and replied, "Yes, they're sitting right in there." The men threw open the door and stomped into Elsie's house like Gestapo agents.

One of the men, a big, pock-marked brute, grabbed Della Raye by the arm and jerked her out of her chair. The other one did the same to Verna. "Get out there to the car," the big man growled, and shoved them out the door.

As the girls neared the car, Della Raye motioned to Verna to get rid of the keys. Verna gave them a quick toss into a high stand of weeds. The men didn't notice.

Back at Partlow, the men took Della Raye and Verna to a waiting Millie Hennessy. The head supervisor was not amused at their escape. The crippled woman folded her arms across her dumpy body, glowered at them over her wire-rimmed glasses, and snapped, "Where are the keys?" The girls shrugged and told her they didn't have them.

"What have y'all done with those keys?" she demanded. With that, they lost their resolve and confessed to throwing them away at Elsie's house. "Get these two back in that car," Miss Hennessy ordered the men, "and don't come back without those keys."

They drove to Elsie's house again, and Verna showed the men where she had thrown the keys. When they returned, Miss Hennessy separated the girls and locked them in the Cross Hall.

Early the next morning, an irate Dr. Woodruff ordered their heads shaved, a common practice with runaways. Runaways normally had to undergo involuntary douches as well, presumably to discourage pregnancy; but because Della Raye and Verna had been gone so short a time, they were spared that degrading procedure.

Mama Herman's cousin Fanny was given the job of shaving their heads. Fanny had always been fond of Della Raye; so instead of shaving her head, she cut her hair short but left it long enough to comb. She knew that Dr. Woodruff was losing his eyesight, and perhaps, thought he wouldn't notice.

When Dr. Woodruff came to the Cross Hall later that morning, he peered through the bars with his schoolmarm righteousness and asked, "Della Raye, did this running away have anything to do with your being considered to work in my home?" Several girls worked as servants and maids in the assistant director's home on the grounds, and Della knew that working there was one of the better jobs at Partlow, but she had no idea that she had been considered for it.

"No, I didn't know anything about that," she replied.

"Well, I had been considering having you work in my home," he said. "I've even talked to Mrs. Woodruff about it, but that's all off now, of course."

Then the doctor frowned, squinted his eyes, and told an attendant to unlock the door. "Step out here," he ordered Della Raye. He reached up and ran his hand over her head. "Why, there's still hair up there!" he exclaimed. "Who did this?" When an assistant informed him that Fanny Herman had cut her hair, the doctor shouted, "Bring Miss Herman here."

While Della Raye stood and listened, Dr. Woodruff gave Fanny Herman a tongue lashing she wouldn't soon forget. Then he dismissed the attendant and told another, "Bring those clippers to me."

Though he could barely see her hair, Dr. Woodruff held Della's head in one hand, the clippers in the other, and shaved her scalp. When he finished, he rubbed her head and said proudly: "I don't think I did too bad a job, did I?"

"No, not for a blind man," Della cracked. Dr. Woodruff scowled, cocked back an arm, and slapped her hard across the face.

Della Raye was shoved back into the tiny cell, this time for a very long stay. In the pale gloom, she sunk to the hard pallet, pulled her knees up under her chin, dropped her shaved head, and wept bitterly. The fetid air smelled of urine and feces, and from somewhere down the line of cages came a high-pitched giggle of lunacy.

CHAPTER SIX

The Edge of Despair

Della Raye was eighteen when she escaped, and had not been outside the gate since the age of four. For less than one hour of freedom, she would pay a high price: four weeks in the Cross Hall—a full month of eating out of tin trays, passing stinking slop jars back and forth, and sitting for endless hours in the dim light that seeped between the bars. And when they did let her out, the punishment wasn't over. She had her head shaved regularly for six more months and wore a heavy denim "sweat dress" as well, public reminders of her great sin.

And if Della had harbored any lingering hopes that Rena Scott might get her out, the escape dashed them completely.

I figured when Rena Scott heard about me running away, it just finished me with her. I never heard from her again.

A new Administration Building went up in 1940, just before the war; but no more would be added until the war ended, five years later. As great numbers of citizens were called into the military, the mental health system became even more short-handed. Partlow and Bryce were no exceptions, but the wartime shortage of workers may have helped Della Raye; she finally left the hated kitchen job.

The farm colony at Bryce Hospital needed help, so Della Raye and several others from Partlow were sent there to pick cotton. She enjoyed riding out the main gate in a car and traveling a few miles to the fields; and after four long years in the kitchen, she didn't mind picking cotton. But she didn't do it well. Being a perfectionist, Della Raye would bend over, pick off a single cotton boll, straighten up, and meticulously clean every bit of the hard pod and stem material from it before carefully placing it in the bag she dragged behind her. No one reprimanded her, but she soon found herself lagging far behind the others. She stopped and watched to see how they did it.

The other patients were picking cotton like mad. Della Raye studied them closely for a few moments, then bent over and started pulling cotton bolls off the stem, rapidly separating the hard parts, stuffing them into the bag, and grabbing another. And like the others, she began cutting her hands to ribbons in the process.

The ones picking ahead of her might have been satisfied with a poor job of cleaning the cotton and ripping their hands to pieces doing it, but to Della Raye it made no sense. She never made it as a cotton picker.

Families were torn apart during the Depression, especially in the South. In a society largely rural, destitute, and uneducated, if one or both parents died, succumbed to alcoholism, or simply disappeared because they could no longer stand the stress, the children often had nowhere to turn. Some were parceled out to relatives; some went to foster homes; and some ended up in places like Partlow and Bryce. A few of the more fortunate would meet their brothers and sisters years later at emotional mid-life reunions, while many never saw their siblings again.

Della's friend Mary Simprish had been torn from her family at an early age; and though Della Raye knew little of Mary's background or how she came to be in Partlow, she had often heard her mention a sister, Annie, to whom she had been close. According to Mary, Annie had been a bright, lively, fun-loving girl. Mary missed her sister terribly and often wondered what had happened to her.

Because Della Raye had become accustomed to working with low-grade patients from her punishment at Partlow, after her failed attempt at picking cotton, they sent her to work in the

Untidy Ward at Bryce. Mary was sent along to help. The girls knew they would have to feed, change, and bathe the badly-deformed and insane; but since the job would allow them to leave the grounds and ride in a car for the mile-and-a-half trek from Partlow to Bryce each day, they looked forward to it.

Bryce Hospital, the quintessential insane asylum, consisted mainly of a single large building that overpowered the rest of the grounds. The building lay half-hidden a few blocks off University Street and could be reached only by a long, oak-lined lane; at the end of which, it loomed, imposing and ominously white. At the center of its three-story expanse stood the administrative section. Topped by a sleek white dome and fronted with tall, commanding columns, the central section sternly anchored the wide wings that extended to its right and left; scores of small windows, covered with iron bars, angrily adorned its entirety. A tall smokestack rose from the utility buildings hidden behind the main structure. The stack cast a long shadow over an ancient, abandoned bastille of civil war vintage, its small barred windows shadowed by the foreboding overhang of the rusted iron roof, still seeming to emit the screams of the vanquished souls who suffered there.

Their first morning at Bryce, an attendant led Della Raye and Mary to the Untidy Ward, unlocked the door, and locked it behind them. The long room held female patients only and looked much the same as the wards at Partlow—colorless, poorly lit, and horribly overcrowded with iron bars covering the windows.

As they started through the ward, an odd assortment of deformed and deranged patients turned to stare at the two girls. This was nothing out of the ordinary, nor was the sight of several women lying on the floor a few yards away. One young woman on the floor caught their attention; however, she was totally naked. She lay on her side, slowly rolling her head back and forth and moving one hand in a circular motion in front of her face while singing to herself, like a little girl at play. As they drew closer, Mary and Della Raye could see that the girl's head was rolling around in a pile of feces. Her hair was filled with the sticky mess, and with an index finger extended directly in front of her face, she drew great swirls in the pile.

Mary and Della shook their heads at the sickening sight and wrinkled up their noses at the smell. Suddenly, Mary grabbed her mouth and went weak, staggering, nearly falling to her knees, an unspeakable horror gripping her face. Della jumped and caught her under her arms.

"What's wrong, Mary?"

Immovably focused on the naked girl, Mary's lips quivered but she could not make a sound. Then slowly she lifted a trembling arm, pointed at the deranged girl, and gasped, "Annie. It's Annie!"

"Your sister?" Della Raye asked incredulously. Mary nodded numbly.

"No! How could it be?"

"I don't know," Mary said, her face gone ashen. "But it's her."

Annie never looked up. She went on drawing circles in the pile and singing her little song.

Dr. Woodruff had run Partlow for twenty years and appeared to have several more vital years left in him. Following complications during surgery in January of 1944, however, he died unexpectedly at the age of fifty-seven. The institution suddenly found itself without a leader, but W. D. Partlow quickly rectified the problem. He elevated his brother, Dr. R. C. Partlow, to the position. To the uninformed, the promotion may have smacked of nepotism, but this was not simply a case of one brother taking care of another. Having worked in the Alabama mental health system for thirty-two years, R. C. Partlow possessed indisputable credentials for the job of assistant director. He had been serving on the staff at Bryce when Dr. Woodruff died.

Not only did R. C. Partlow's qualifications read well on paper, he proved a capable leader who would artfully guide the institution through two more decades of impossibly hard times. Though he remained the only physician on staff for much of his tenure, somehow he found time to solicit contributions, enlist volunteer help, and seek out sources of used furniture and appliances.

Like his famous brother, this Dr. Partlow was imaginative and resourceful. Unlike his brother, he was a humble man. Although he found himself charged with running a large, overcrowded institution with an untrained staff and terribly inadequate funding, R. C. Partlow demonstrated a genuine concern for his patients.

When she was no longer needed at Bryce, Della Raye moved to another full-time job that would last several years—the sewing room. The work tended to be repetitive and boring, but with her natural dexterity, Della found it more satisfying than anything she had done before.

Along with about thirty other patients, she worked in a huge underground room, filled with sewing machines. Located in the basement of the Number Two Building, the sewing room comprised a sweatshop where two people could turn out a hundred sheets before noon. After Della Raye learned to make simple things such as sheets and pillowcases, she quickly moved on to more complicated pieces. All of the sewing machines were operated by a foot treadle with the exception of a single machine that had been electrified. The attendants soon acknowledged Della's superior skills and assigned her to the electric machine. This made some of the other girls jealous, but as always Della took advantage of an opportunity to learn. Soon she could make every item of clothing worn by Partlow patients, and in every size conceivable. Occasionally, she made a special piece with flowered sacks saved from the kitchen, and remembered the wonderful dress that Massie had once fashioned for her by hand, the one she had worn less than five minutes.

Della was eighteen when she went to the sewing room, and though she would never hate the job as she had the kitchen,

Della Raye in her teen years at Partlow

Della Raye two years after her release (1951)

A middle-aged Della Raye

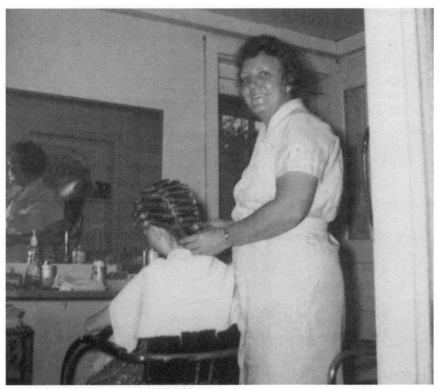

Della Raye styling her stepdaughter Patsy's hair

Ruby Rogers, Della Raye's mother

Della Raye's uncle, Richard Rogers

Richard Rogers

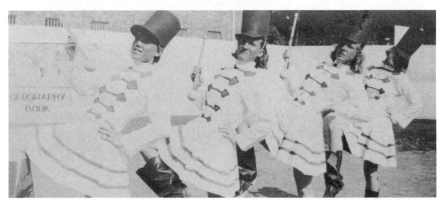

Della Raye (third from left) and other Partlow inmates on display (showing visitors how well-off they were)

Della Raye (far right) posing with other Partlow patients

Willa Mae Kilpatrick at Partlow

Grace Wright (front)

Partlow patients on Schoolhouse stage

A group of Partlow patients posing for a picture, all were considered retarded.

Lula Clemons

Massie and Della Raye, after her release

Massie at Partlow

Partlow employees (from left to right)
Annie Stokes, Kate Nevins, and Massie

Rena Scott (left) and Della Raye at Partlow

(From left to right) James, Kenny, and
Anna Lee Dockery

Margaret (Maggie) Williams at Partlow

Maggie Williams (far right) on Schoolhouse stage

Partlow employees

Partlow employee

Myrta Poe

Floyd Hughes

Floyd Hughes

Floyd Hughes and Della Raye, shortly after their marriage

(From left to right) Butch and Donny Hughes

Ruby holding Donny (left), Floyd Hughes (right), and unknown child

Richard Rogers (left) and Donny (right)

Della Raye and Donny, approximately 1962

Ruby Rogers, visiting Della Raye's house

Frank and Ruby Rogers in Collinsville, Alabama nursing home.

Frank (left) and Ruby (far right) in nursing home, shortly before Ruby's death

Dovie Rogers' headstone in pauper cemetery at Partlow, about the size of a brick (most headstones were almost buried)

(From left to right) Frank, Della Raye, and Massie (1980s)

Della Raye with the first doll she ever had, given to her by her grandchildren, at age 73

Della Raye with author Gary Penley at her home in Tuscaloosa, Alabama

Della Raye at the door of her beauty shop (1999)

Della Raye's home (1999)

Della Raye and Gary Penley at Partlow's patient cemetery

Partlow sign on University Street as it stands today

Old Administration Building at Partlow

Remnants of Partlow's barbed-wire fence

Enclosed cage from which patients watch ball games

Old buildings at the site of Boys Colony

Partlow's old, main, front gate—still standing but unused

it did become tedious. She still prayed for her freedom and tried to remain hopeful, but always in the back of her mind lay the haunting fear that she might never leave Partlow.

Della had more free time in the evenings now than she'd had before, and she spent much of it reading the Bible. She also helped take care of the books in the library, many of which she read a second or third time. Massie bought books for her too, as well as borrowing them from friends and checking them out of the city library. And one evening Massie sneaked her an ice cream cone, the first one Della Raye had ever seen. She licked it, tasted its richness, and savored every bite. She couldn't imagine what it would be like to enjoy such wonders every day.

In the fall of 1944, R. C. Partlow received a request for Della's release. Mrs. Louis Brady of Hope Hull, Alabama, wrote:

> "It has come to my knowledge you have a girl in your school named Della Rae Rogers. I would like to know if there is a chance of getting this girl out to make her home with me. My health is very bad and I need someone with me at all times. I am sure we can make her happy. My husband and I are willing to give her a permanent home, buy her clothes, etc. and accept all responsibility in general. We can also furnish the very best references for my husband and myself. We understand perfectly the responsibility we are taking upon ourselves."

Dr. Partlow denied Mrs. Brady's request. The very next day he sent the following reply:

> "Here where she has constant care and strict supervision she ordinarily does not give much trouble, usually being pleasant and agreeable. She, however, gets troublesome here, at times has a rather ugly temper and is rather stubborn. She has become accustomed to the regularity of the Institution and we do not believe that she could make proper social adjustment outside. She will always be feebleminded and childish."

Dr. Partlow's reason for depicting Della Raye as childish, troublesome, and irrevocably feebleminded remains difficult to discern, as his statement would stand in stark contrast to later assessments that he himself would make.

Della never learned the origin of the idea, but one day Massie smiled at her and said, "I've got a surprise for you, Della Raye. I think you're going to like it."

"What's that, Massie?" she asked. "What kind of surprise?"

"They're going to put in a beauty shop, here at Partlow."

"A beauty shop!" Della said excitedly. "Where?"

"Upstairs in the Main Building, right beside the marking room," Massie said. "And I'm going to be in charge of it."

"Who's going to work in it?" Della asked eagerly.

"You are," Massie said. "You and Mary are going to work in it." Mary had been learning hair styling from Della, and Massie knew that the two of them would work well together.

"Oh, that's so exciting!" Della said. "Have you told Mary?"

"No," Massie answered with a grin. "I thought I'd let you do that." Della gave her a quick hug and ran off to tell Mary the news.

Della Raye and Mary did two permanents and two shampoos and sets every morning, then went back to their regular jobs in the afternoon. Having learned her skills on her own with neither a teacher nor tools to work with, Della Raye saw the beauty shop as a personal accomplishment. And working there provided a nice break from the tedium of the sewing room as well.

A Birmingham newspaper called it: "Partlow's beauty parlor, where two girls proudly work." The shop was equipped with two chairs, two rinse sinks, and two hair-curling machines. A curling machine consisted of a large metal hood fastened to the back of a chair by a bracket that elevated it over a woman's head. Like an oversized bullet-shaped helmet, the hood appeared to rivet the woman to the chair. A thick electrical cord connected the machine to a wall socket, while a maze of shorter cords emanated from the hood like the tentacles of an octopus. Because the permanent solution required heat to dry, each cord was clipped to a metal curler in the woman's hair. When the operator flipped a switch, the curlers heated up the hair and dried the solution.

Most of the patients enjoyed getting their hair done in a real beauty shop, but it turned out to be less than a pleasant experience for one of them.

A retarded girl named Ginny came into the shop one day and asked for a permanent. Ginny was sincere and quite likable, but because she was known to be overly afraid of many things, Della Raye and Mary were reluctant to work on her. They told the squeamish girl she would have to ask Massie.

When Ginny approached Massie about getting a permanent, the girl found her reluctant as well. "They'd have to put a bunch of curlers in your hair and hook you up to that machine with all those wires," Massie told her. "Then they'd put that big thing over your head. How do you think you'd like that?"

"That'd be okay," Ginny assured her. "I want my hair to look purty like the other girls' does."

Ginny appeared to have resolved her fear, or at least it seemed so to Massie. The simple girl was anxious to have her hair done and Massie was soft-hearted; in the end, she agreed to let Della give Ginny a permanent.

Early the next morning, Ginny walked into the shop, her simple face beaming. Della Raye and Mary were not beaming. "You're sure about this now?" Della asked her.

"Oh, yeah," Ginny replied. "Massie said it was okay. Now I'm gonna be purty like the other girls."

With a sigh of resignation, Della ushered Ginny into a chair, leaned her head back over the rinse sink, and shampooed her hair. The girl's eyes danced in anticipation of how pretty she was going to be. Della sat her up, rolled about thirty metal curlers into her hair, and began snapping the electrical cords onto them. Looking somewhat fearful, Ginny sat stiffly and winced each time a clamp snapped shut on a curler.

When all the cords were attached, Ginny looked like an electrified bride of Frankenstein—a very nervous one. With the hood hovering over her head like a medieval instrument of torture, she sat rigid and straight, her eyes rolling around as she tried to get a glimpse of the cords attached to the curlers in her hair. Looking as if she might be waiting for a hurricane to hit, Mary watched worriedly from the opposite chair.

"Are you okay?" Della asked. Ginny nodded semi-bravely, but quickly stopped when the nodding rattled the cords. "All right. It's time to put this hood over your head," Della Raye said. Ginny's eyes rolled wildly in their sockets as Della fitted the hood over her head. She made no sound.

"There now," Della said, and flipped on the switch.

Looking like a raccoon trapped under a washtub, Ginny peered fearfully from under the hood. Nothing happened for a minute or so, then the curlers began to heat up. Feeling the heat on her head, Ginny closed her eyes. The curlers grew hotter and hotter, and a hissing, singeing sound issued from under the hood. Ginny opened her eyes widely and clamped her jaws. Amplified inside the hood, the singeing sounded like bacon frying on her head.

A thin trail of steam curled from under the hood, a shadowy wisp of smoke directly above Ginny's fearfully upturned eyes. Her mouth flew open and she filled the shop with a scream. Shrieking in terror, the girl leaped up, frantically tore the hood from her head, and tried to run. She could not. The cords held her in place. Ginny jerked the chair sideways and lost her balance as the cords yanked her hair violently. Squalling and clawing like a wounded animal, she fell to the floor on her face, pulling the hood and chair over on top of her.

Della Raye and Mary jumped on the struggling girl's back, screaming for help as they fought to subdue her. Several attendants came running and held Ginny down while Della rushed to unplug the machine. The metal curlers were too hot to touch, and while Ginny screamed and writhed in the attendants' grip, Mary and Della burned their fingers unsnapping the wire from each one.

When they finally managed to release all the cords from her head, they forced Ginny's back against the wall and talked to her soothingly until she stopped screaming. "I'm sorry, Ginny," Della said. "We told you this might not work out, you know."

The girl didn't answer, just rolled her eyes fearfully at the alien machine. The hood that had attacked her so viciously lay lifeless on the floor, the dread curlers cold, the cords benign. She would never go near it again.

Della Raye recalls vividly the day an attendant handed her a postcard addressed to: Della Raye Rogers, Partlow State School, Tuscaloosa, Alabama. In her eighteen years at Partlow, she had never received a single piece of mail. The card turned out to be only a simple note sent by a friendly attendant away on vacation, but she treasured it more than the thoughtful attendant could have imagined.

Besides the total absence of mail, during her years of incarceration, Della Raye had never had a single visitor either. Then one day in late 1947, when she was twenty-three, an attendant called out, "Della, you've got some visitors." She followed the attendant to the rotunda, her face asking the obvious question as they walked. Surely it must be a mistake. They got her name mixed up with someone else's. The visitors couldn't be hers.

She quickly recognized Dickie Jr., lurched crookedly in his bib overalls and looking at her shyly with a simple grin, but not the tall, middle-aged man standing beside him. Worn overalls hung loosely on his lean frame, and he held an ancient felt hat in his long, skinny hands; and though she didn't know him, something about his narrow face seemed familiar.

"Hello, Della Raye," the lanky man said. "I guess you don't know who I am. I'm your Uncle Richard."

Della stopped short, her eyes widening in disbelief. She said nothing, just looked him up and down; then the family resemblance became clear. She stood and stared at him until the silence hung heavy in the air. Finally, as Richard fidgeted and Dickie Jr. gazed aimlessly about, she spoke.

"I never expected to see you again."

"It sure is nice to see you, Della Raye," Richard chimed. "How you been?" She didn't reply. Her entire childhood was gone, yet he sounded as if no time had passed at all. "I was here seein' about Frank comin' to live with us and work with me on the farm," Richard said. "So I thought I'd bring Dickie Jr. and stop by to see you too."

"You're going to take Frank home with you?" Della Raye asked.

"Well, I wanted to," he replied, "but it don't look like it's gonna work out."

"Why are you coming to see me now?" she asked him bluntly. "You never even wrote me a letter in nineteen years."

Richard stood quietly for a moment, avoiding her eyes, then turned and walked out. Della Raye and Dickie Jr. stood in silence. After a few minutes, Richard returned; he was carrying a bottle of soda in his hand, which he handed to Dickie Jr. When Dickie held up the bottle and looked at it dumbly, Richard tilted his head back and raised his hand, showing him how to drink from the bottle. Dickie smiled merrily, lifted the bottle, tipped it to his mouth, and jammed the neck far down his throat.

Della Raye ignored Dickie Jr. as he threw the bottle across the rotunda, choked, sputtered, and coughed up sprays of soda he had forced down the wrong tube. "You said taking Frank home with you wasn't going to work out. Why not?" she asked Richard.

"Well, it sure is strange," he said. "I figured Frank would be good help on the farm, what with him workin' at that Colony and all. But all he could talk about was the pigs and chickens and cows he'd have to leave behind, the ones he takes care of at the Colony. Dr. Partlow said he just didn't think it'd work, and he won't let him go."

Why did Uncle Richard come to visit Della Raye after nineteen years? And why did he bring Dickie Jr. with him that day? Perhaps, he also hoped to take Dickie home to help him on the farm, though it probably didn't take him long to figure out why that wouldn't work.

Unbeknown to Della Raye, Richard also attempted to secure her release that day. Dr. Partlow was obviously concerned about her uncle's character as well his motives, and he wouldn't allow that either.

Frances Woodruff, the compassionate welfare worker who had arranged for Della Raye's failed adoption two decades earlier, had become the Director of Public Welfare in Athens, Alabama. Dr. Partlow wrote to her the same day of Richard's visit.

> "My dear Mrs. Woodruff: "As your records probably already show we have in the School from your county several of the Rogers family and we are writing you particularly concerning Della Ray Rogers. She is the highest grade mentality of any of the kin in the Rogers family here . . . Her uncle, Mr. Richard Rogers, is here this morning visiting her and other relatives. He is interested in taking her home and it may be that he is wanting to take her for help in the family instead of their being of assistance to Della Ray. That always has to be taken into consideration."

Although Dr. Partlow refused to release Della Raye to her Uncle Richard, records indicate that the institution was beginning to feel pressure concerning its rigid release policy. In an interview two years earlier, R. C. Partlow had given the results of a study of eight hundred and thirty-eight patients as to their fitness for parole. Based on the study, he felt that one hundred and four of them could be released with a good chance of maintaining themselves in the community "provided they were not fertile."

Della Raye was likely included in that group of one hundred and four, but only if she was rendered infertile. The governor may have forced them to stop the practice of sterilization a decade before, but Partlow still held solidly to eugenic beliefs.

Quoted in the June, 1945 issue of *The Journal of the Medical Association of the State of Alabama,* R. C. Partlow addressed parole considerations. Explaining that primary amentia was of the hereditary type and secondary amentia was that caused by the environment, Dr. Partlow said of his potential parolees:

". . . most of those who are considered for parole are of the primary endogenous or hereditary type of amentia and should not leave the institution having the ability to reproduce others of their kind."

After nearly two decades of incarceration, years in which she had demonstrated intelligence and abilities beyond those of many of her captors, Della Raye remained condemned due to feeblemindedness in her family line.

While capable people languished behind locked doors and barbed wire fences, overcrowding continued to the point that many patients had no bed. The ones who didn't slept on floors. Each night a row of mattresses was laid down the center aisle of the ward to accommodate the overflow. A patient could not walk to the bathroom without stepping on others.

Despite the eugenic inertia, the official attitude toward Della Raye appeared to be shifting, however slightly. Dr. Partlow had the good sense to suspect Richard's motives when he sought her release, but instead of the dismal mental prognosis the doctor had portrayed to Mrs. Brady(the lady who had sought her release three years before), now he told the welfare director that Della should possibly be let out on a trial basis if a "proper, caring environment" could be found. And he went even further; instead of the stubborn, troublesome girl he had described to Mrs. Brady—a girl who had an ugly temper and did "a little work"—now he depicted Della Raye as industrious, well-behaved, pleasant, and agreeable. And though no test exists in her record to document the change, according to Dr. Partlow, her IQ had somehow jumped to 72.

Della Raye was never told of Mrs. Brady's attempt to obtain her release or about the subsequent denial stating that she would always be feebleminded and childish; nor did she know of her uncle's attempt to sign her out, or of the denial based on his questionable motives.

She also remained unaware of Dr. Partlow's statement that he might consider her for parole if a caring environment could be found. But all the hopeful talk and supposed good intentions mattered little anyway—Uncle Richard was the only relative who could legally sign Della out, and Dr. Partlow wouldn't allow him to do it.

Della's job in the sewing room ended in February of 1948. She'd been there four years, about the same amount of time she had spent in the kitchen. She still worked mornings in the beauty shop, but now spent her afternoons working in the assistant director's residence on the grounds.

In all her years in the kitchen, Della Raye never had the opportunity to learn to cook. She hoped to gain those skills working in Dr. Partlow's home, but she didn't get the chance there either. She was assigned to work as a maid.

Della may not have learned to cook at Dr. Partlow's house, but she certainly took advantage of the cooking. She and the other girls who worked there had access to better food and more of it than they had ever known. Della Raye started the job reasonably trim, but one year later she weighed a hundred and seventy-five pounds.

The seeming hopelessness of her life may have contributed to the weight problem. A bit of her natural fire, and even the hair-trigger defiance, seemed to be ebbing; and more and more, she found herself despondent.

"Don't give up hope, Della Raye," Massie told her. "God is still watching out for you. Keep praying for your freedom."

"I do pray for my freedom, every night," Della said. "But I don't know how it could ever happen. I've got no people out there that care about me. There's no one to get me out."

CHAPTER SEVEN

The Miracle

A year after Richard and Dickie's surprise visit, Della received another. In the fall of 1948, a well-dressed, educated woman drove onto the grounds in an expensive car, walked into the Administration Building, and asked to see Della Raye. The woman, who gave her name as Houston, claimed to be a relative of Della's. Her claim of family relationship aroused Dr. Partlow's suspicion, but he allowed the visit.

"Hello, Della Raye," the woman said when Della entered the rotunda. "My name is Elizabeth Houston. I'm your cousin." Della thought this strange; she had never heard of any such cousin nor had she ever in her life talked with someone as well-dressed as Miss Houston.

The worldly woman sat down and chatted with her easily, but Della remained cautious. When Miss Houston asked questions about her childhood and her life at Partlow, she gave short, vague answers. The woman got her total attention, however, when she asked, "Della Raye, if you had a chance to get out of this place, would you take it?"

After a moment's surprise, Della replied eagerly, "Oh, yes. I've been praying for freedom all my life."

"Good. That's what I needed to know," Miss Houston said. Then she stood up to leave and said something even more confusing: "We just might be able to make that happen." As Della sat puzzling over her supposed cousin's statements, Miss Houston smiled and said, "Take care of yourself, Della Raye," and walked out.

Edna Coen, Partlow's imperious personnel manager, had taken notice of Elizabeth Houston when she came in and asked to visit Della Raye. Coen thought the woman looked familiar, but could not recall how she knew her. Sitting in her office a few days later, Coen suddenly remembered where she had seen the woman.

Stocky, authoritative, and stern as a Nazi, Edna Coen was a coldly efficient manager and fiercely loyal to her boss, R. C. Partlow. She marched directly to his office with the news. "Remember that Houston woman who came to see Della Raye Rogers the other day?" Coen said. The doctor nodded. "I thought she looked familiar, and I finally figured out who she is. She's a secretary for James McCollum, an attorney here in Tuscaloosa." Dr. Partlow looked thoughtful for a moment, then thanked her.

For a while Della Raye continued to puzzle over the strange visit from Elizabeth Houston, but as time passed and she heard nothing else, she thought little more of it. She'd been deluded by false hopes once, and wouldn't let it happen again. Then one day about three months later, early in January of 1949, an attendant came through the ward looking for her.

"Dr. Partlow wants to see you out in the rotunda, Della Raye," the attendant said.

"Dr. Partlow?" she thought to herself. "Why would he want to see me?"

R. C. Partlow appeared tense as she walked into the rotunda. "Hello, Della Raye," he said with a businesslike air. "How are you?"

"I'm okay, Dr. Partlow," she replied warily.

The doctor wasted no time. He looked her directly in the eye and asked, "How would you like to have your freedom, Della Raye?"

There was that question again. After a moment of surprise, Della replied, "Why, I'd love to have my freedom, Dr. Partlow. I've prayed for it all my life."

"You have a chance to get your freedom, Della Raye. We intend to let you go home with your uncle, Richard Rogers. I've written and told him to come and get you as soon as he can."

Della was stunned. "Why would he want to get me out?" she said.

Dr. Partlow ignored her question. Instead he asked, "Do you remember when that woman named Houston came to visit you a few months back, Della Raye?"

"Yes, I remember," she replied.

"She was dressed in expensive clothing and driving a brand new car. Did you really think that woman was kin to you?" he said.

"How would I know if she was my cousin or not?" Della Raye answered. "Any more than I know that this man you say is coming to get me is really my uncle. My uncle put me in here and didn't come to see me for nineteen years, then last year here this man comes out of the blue and brings Dickie Jr. with him. Then this Houston woman shows up and tells me I might get out. All this doesn't make any sense to me, Dr. Partlow."

"I assure you the man is your uncle, Della Raye, and I'll tell you what's going on. Some people here in Tuscaloosa have started a legal action to try and get you out. It's called habeas corpus. We're afraid the people doing this don't have your best interests in mind, and we want to make sure that you go to your uncle's home. We understand he lives in the northern part of the state, somewhere up near Athens."

"Yes, he lived there before he put me in here," Della Raye said. "Who are these people who want to get me out, Dr. Partlow?"

"We don't know who they are," he replied. "But we don't feel that they could give you a good home if they were to get you out. It's better for you to go up to Athens with your uncle, Della Raye. You'll be better off living away from here and away from those people. They would probably just get you in trouble. And something else—you can not come back to Tuscaloosa ever again. If we let you go with your uncle, you can never return to Tuscaloosa. Do you understand?"

Della Raye nodded. "I understand."

On December 21, 1948, three weeks prior to Della Raye's conversation with Dr. Partlow, attorney James McCollum had filed the following petition with the honorable Reuben H. Wright, Judge of the Circuit Court of Tuscaloosa County, Alabama:

PETITION FOR A WRIT OF HABEAS CORPUS FOR THE RELEASE OF DELLA RAY ROGERS FROM PARTLOW STATE SCHOOL:

"Your petitioner, Mrs. Janice Loeman [not the actual name on the petition], would respectfully show and represent that Della Ray Rogers is imprisoned or deprived of her liberty in the Partlow State School at Tuscaloosa, Alabama, by one R. C. Partlow as acting Assistant Superintendent of said Partlow State School by virtue of a warrant or commitment issued by party or parties unknown to your petitioner and a copy of said warrant or commitment has been demanded and refused.

"Your petitioner further alleges that the warrant or commitment was issued under circumstances not allowed by law in that no offense had been committed by the said Della Ray Rogers and that said Della Ray Rogers is detained and restrained and deprived of her liberty unlawfully; that said Della Ray Rogers has never been insane and if she has ever been insane she has now been restored to sanity: and said Della Ray Rogers has requested your petitioner to assist her in securing her release.

"WHEREFORE, Your petitioner prays that a writ of habeas corpus issue immediately directed to the said R. C. Partlow as acting Assistant Superintendent of said Partlow State School commanding him to bring the body of the said Della Ray Rogers before your Honor at a time and place to be by your Honor appointed together with the cause of the detention of the said Della Ray Rogers."

The following day, Judge Wright issued an order to Dr. Partlow. Officially served by the sheriff of Tuscaloosa County, the order stated:

> "You are hereby commanded to have the body of the said Della Ray Rogers alleged to be detained by you with the cause of such detention, before me as Judge of the Circuit Court of Tuscaloosa County, Alabama, on the 26th day of January, 1949."

Janice Loeman, the petitioner who had filed for the writ of habeas corpus, was a mystery person. A state attorney assured Dr. Partlow that the name probably was fictitious. The name was not fictitious; however, and it is unclear whether Dr. Partlow ever figured out that Janice Loeman was Homer Duncan's sister.

The Partlow people were obviously certain of one thing— they wanted no part of showcasing Della Raye in Judge Wright's court. Under oath, they would be forced to admit that they had been holding her prisoner for twenty years, after which they would have to try and convince the judge that she was mentally retarded. Evidently, the prospect of such a debacle did not rest easy on their minds. A great flurry of letters ensued.

Dr. Partlow had previously stated that Della Raye might be allowed to go out on a trial basis if a "proper, caring environment" could be found. And although at the time he had forbidden Richard to take custody of her, suddenly Richard's place became that caring environment the institution had been looking for. Dr. Partlow wrote to Richard and told him to come and get her "promptly within receipt of this letter," or within a maximum of ten days. "Any day that you come for her she can go along with you," he promised.

Dr. Partlow also wrote to Frances Woodruff, the welfare director, telling her of his decision to release Della Raye to Richard and explaining that "certain persons around Tuscaloosa had been making efforts to get her out and for no good reason."

And evidently, Della's intelligence was still magically on the upswing. In another letter informing an Athens County judge of her release, Partlow described Della Raye as ". . . one of our highest grade girls, was a borderline case between a high grade moron and a dull normal . . ."

With Della's release in place and Richard scheduled to come for her, Dr. Partlow called Judge Wright and explained that they had managed to find her a home. Apparently this appeased the judge, as he then canceled the habeas corpus hearing. The sigh of relief emanating from Partlow must have been audible for miles.

As for the "certain persons around Tuscaloosa" who had hired the lawyer to secure Della's release, it seems likely that Dr. Partlow would have figured out it was Homer. If he did come to that conclusion, he never put it in writing.

An interesting flurry of changes. Not only had Della Raye's IQ spontaneously jumped into the seventies during her last year at Partlow, but her mental diagnosis also made a rapid climb from imbecile to high-grade moron to "dull normal," whatever the meaning of that strange term may be. One might say she was gaining intelligence before the judges' eyes. That would be incorrect, however—no judge had seen Della Raye, and it appears that Partlow had been doing everything possible to ensure that the situation remained that way.

Della Raye knew nothing of the ongoing events—the people involved, the accusations, the threats, or the rapid scrambling and covering of tracks. She only knew she had received some strange visits, and that because of something called habeas corpus she was going to be free, none of which she understood in the least.

On the morning of January 17, 1949, Richard came for her. He surely didn't comprehend it all either; he only knew that he had once tried unsuccessfully to get her out and now he had somehow accomplished it.

Both Partlow brothers met with Della Raye and Richard the morning of her departure. R. C. Partlow and the director, his powerful brother W. D., talked to the two of them at length about the adjustment she would have to face in order to make it on the outside. The Partlows also explained that as a parolee she would be on institutional probation for six months, a period during which she could be returned at any time she was unable to get along with those in custody of her or if for any other reason her parole wasn't working. A record of the meeting that morning reflects a sincere concern for Della's welfare on the part of both Dr. Partlows. Whatever their thoughts regarding her true mental capacity may have been, the doctors knew full well that they were turning a young woman out into the world who had been institutionalized virtually all her life.

Della Raye nodded and tried to listen to the doctors' advice but mostly she sat in stunned silence, the happenings of that day beyond her comprehension. Then all too soon, after a hug from Massie and a promise to write, quick goodbyes from Lula, Grace, Mary, Mama Leonard, Maggie Williams, and others, she was on her way.

Looking down the length of the drab ward for the last time, Della Raye shook with emotion. Every night for twenty years, she laid in one of those metal cots and prayed for her freedom—her only dream—yet now that the time had finally come, she felt no elation whatsoever. Partlow may have been a mental institution, but it was the only home she had ever known.

It should have been the happiest day of my life, but it was the saddest.

Richard led Della Raye out the main gate, the same one he had delivered her to a lifetime ago. Outside the gate she hesitated, then stopped. Slowly, she turned her head to the right, and then to the left. Gazing up and down the long street, an unspeakable fear gripped her. An entire world lay out there, alien and unknown, the fear of which overwhelmed her very perception. In disturbing contrast to what she had always dreamed, this outside world appeared colorless, featureless, and frightening beyond belief.

Richard understood none of this, nor did he seem to care. "Come on, Della Raye," he said impatiently. "We got a bus to catch, and a long ways to go."

In the bus station, Della Raye sat on a bench, bowed and fearfully still, a paper grocery bag clutched tightly against her faded cotton dress. Everything she owned was in the paper bag, and she had not a penny to her name. Like a lost, frightened animal, she slowly raised her head and cast wary eyes around the smoke-filled room. Rows of dirty benches, like the one she sat on, crowded its tobacco-stained floors; a murmur of voices echoed off high, cracked walls; shadowy spittoons lurked in musty corners. Unshaven men with blackened teeth and hollow eyes stared blankly; stringy-haired women tended ragged children crawling the floor.

And everyone seemed to be looking at her.

Richard sat beside her, slouched against the back of the bench, hat perched jauntily on one side of his head, gazing around the room with an air of cocky disdain. Della slowly turned toward him, looked up at his craggy face and asked, "What kind of place is this, Uncle Richard?"

"It's a bus station, Della Raye," he replied with annoyance. "Ever town in Alabama's got one."

"How would I know what a bus station is?" she said. "I haven't been outside Partlow since you put me in there, twenty years ago." He didn't answer. Della Raye leaned forward against her paper sack and began to cry. Richard looked around the room, embarrassed, and shook his head in disgust.

In an ironic coincidence, five girls had escaped from Partlow that morning. While Della Raye and Richard sat waiting for their bus, three male attendants came running through the station, looking for the escapees. One of them, the pockmarked brute who had taken Della back when she escaped, recognized her. "Aren't you Della Raye Rogers?" the big man asked.

"Yes, I am," she replied through tears, then added defensively, "I got released today. I'm going home with my uncle."

"Yeah, I know about that," the man replied. "We're looking for some girls that escaped. Have you seen any of them come through here?"

"No, I haven't," Della Raye answered. "And I wouldn't tell you if I had. I hope you never find them."

Della cried nearly all the way to Athens, a bus ride of several hours. A lifetime ago she had wept in fear of going to Partlow; now she wept in fear of leaving it. Richard's patience wore thin. "My God, Della Raye," he said with disgust. "You're outta that place now. What're you carryin' on about?"

She looked at him intently, her reddened eyes pleading for understanding, then turned away without answering.

I had a funny feeling about my uncle, and it turned out to be right. I cried all that day.

Della was wiping her eyes as they stepped off the bus in Athens, a small town that served as the hub of a widespread agricultural community. They left the station quickly and walked out of town on a narrow dirt road. Gripping the paper bag tightly against her chest, Della Raye fell in behind her uncle.

"How far do we have to go?" she asked.

"Nine miles," he said. "And we better get steppin' if we want to get there before dark. Looks like it might come up a storm tonight." Della quickened her pace, and broke into tears again.

Richard stretched his gangly legs and walked ahead while Della clutched her bag and followed, weeping and wailing miserably. Uphill and downhill they walked, passing mile after mile of fields, meadows, and woods, but Della Raye hardly noticed. To her overloaded mind the world still looked colorless and featureless, the same as it had all day long, and the dusty road seemed endless. They never caught sight of a single house and as Richard had predicted, storm clouds began to gather overhead.

Just before nightfall, Richard pointed to a distant, dilapidated house crouching at the edge of a field. "That's my place," he said. Six ragged boys, ranging in age from five to fifteen, ran across the field toward them. A hundred yards away, the boys stopped and stared uncertainly at Della. "This here's Della Raye," Richard hollered to them. "She's gonna be stayin' with us." None of the boys moved or said a word, neither to their father nor Della Raye.

Richard's wife, Cora, met them at the door. Though she was his second wife, Cora had been only thirteen when Richard married her. She might have once been pretty; a vestige of happier times still showed in her blue eyes, but even that wouldn't last much longer. Her eyes, mimicking her overworked and undernourished body, were well on the way to becoming hollowed and weary from the strain of a life that was draining her of all pride and care. She was small and thin, the skin on her face weather-worn and leather-tough, and her home-cut hair had seldom seen soap. A faded feed-sack dress hung loosely on her spindly frame. A three-year-old girl, her face so filthy it masked her features, clung to her legs.

Della looked deeply into Cora's eyes and found compassion there. The worn woman smiled tenderly, held out a small, rough hand and said, "Come in, Della Raye. Y'all had a long walk, but it looks like you beat the storm home anyhow."

The house was one of a great number of sharecropper shacks that Richard and Cora had occupied. Like all the others, it belonged to the landowner. Small, swaybacked, loose, and leaky, the unpainted hovel comprised a kitchen, living room, and two little bedrooms, all clinging together in hopeless disrepair. The inside smelled of unwashed bodies, kitchen grease, and dust, and the rough plank floor was as dirty as the ground outside.

Cora took Della's sack and led her to the table, then struck a match and lit a kerosene lamp, their only source of light.

"Sit down," she said kindly, "and I'll bring you and Richard some supper." Then glancing quickly around the room, Cora dispersed the crowd of staring kids. "You boys get on outta here now; quit standin' around starin' at Della Raye. She ain't some kinda freak, you know; she's your cousin. And she's gonna be stayin' with us, at least for now anyhow."

Richard hadn't offered to buy lunch for Della that day, nor had he eaten himself. Weak from hunger and exhaustion, she dropped limply into a chair as Richard fell into another. Cora brought two steaming bowls of black-eyed peas and set them on the homemade table. Della polished off the bowl quickly and could have eaten several more, but none was offered. Richard ate only one bowl himself.

Apportioning a family of nine into two bedrooms had always been difficult, and now there were ten. The little girl, Bonnie, slept with Richard and Cora, while the two oldest boys, thirteen and fifteen, slept on the floor in the same room. Della Raye and the four younger boys slept in the second bedroom, which had two double beds. The boys all had to crowd into one and relinquish the other to Della Raye. They started to protest the arrangement to Cora, but under Richard's melting glare, they quickly shut up.

Having nowhere to undress, Della climbed into bed in her clothes. When the boys did the same, she assumed they were doing it in deference to her. She had not yet learned that they always slept in their clothes.

Although Della Raye felt overcome with exhaustion after eating, in this strange new world, she found herself unable to sleep. In the opposite bed, where two of the boys lay with their heads in one direction and two the other, she could hear them struggling to stake claims for themselves. "Scoot over," one would say, "you're pushing me off." Then, "Hey! Get your damn toe outta my mouth!"

Later that night the storm hit. Bolts of lightning pierced the blackness and danced across the fields, lighting up the windows in shattering brilliance. Thunder cracked close in, as the wind howled and moaned and tore at every loose shingle and board on the house.

A deafening explosion of thunder shook their beds. "Did y'all hear that?" one of the younger boys asked fearfully.

"Yeah, I heard it," answered another. "How in hell couldn't you hear it?!"

"I'm scared," the younger one said. "I'm really scared."

Della Raye had heard storms at Partlow, of course, but the buildings there had felt solid and secure. Richard's house was dangerously thin, and the boys' fear infectious. As their terror permeated the air, her own mounted beyond control. Coupled with the arduous day she had just endured, the violent storm overwhelmed her. She burst into tears.

As Della Raye lay on her back wailing uncontrollably, one of the boys broke. "I'm getting' the hell outta here!" he said. "I'm goin' in with Mom and Dad." The boy leaped out of bed and ran from the room, the others scrambled after him.

Finding all seven children crowded into their tiny bedroom, Richard and Cora got up and herded them into the living room. With a clutch of kids pressing closely around, they sat by a flickering kerosene lamp and watched the jagged lightning light up the night and listened to the thunder roll like cannon fire from one horizon to the other.

Between claps of thunder they could hear Della Raye crying alone, and she could hear them. Cora looked at Richard with a worried brow. "Don't you think we ought to bring her in here with us?" she asked him.

"No. Leave her alone," he said. "She ain't done nothin' but squall all day."

CHAPTER EIGHT

Frail Freedom

The South suffered more than its share of poverty during the Depression, after which the region contributed a great deal of its manpower to the war effort. By 1949, however, the post-war boom had enabled some of the more ambitious to begin upgrading their lives. Not Richard. He just had more kids.

Many rural homes had no bathrooms at the time; Richard didn't even have an outhouse. The entire family, kids and grownups alike, simply walked off into the woods to relieve themselves. When Della Raye asked Cora what they used for toilet paper, she was horrified but not particularly surprised at the answer: "We ain't got any," Cora said. "We just use sticks, corncobs, or whatever we can find."

Richard ruled the family. A slovenly patriarch who proudly presided over his own squalor, he seldom spoke to his children and wasted no affection on any of them. The kids wore no shoes, in warm weather no shirts as well, and a single set of denim overalls lasted each of them a week. Each Saturday morning the boys got a bath and a clean set of overalls to wear day and night until the following Saturday. And though neither Cora nor the children wore underwear, Richard did. He was the only member of the family who owned underwear.

The landowner always got his money's worth out of Richard. A hard worker, he arose every morning at four o'clock sharp and went to the fields. And because the older boys had to work with him, the rest of the family got up at that time as well.

Breakfast consisted of the same thing every morning—hoe-cake, an unsweetened bread cooked in a skillet, and sawmill gravy, a viscous concoction made from flour and grease in the same skil-let. One simply broke off a piece of hoecake with their fingers and covered it with gravy. They had no meat to go with the hoecake and gravy; but this mixture made a tasty country breakfast, that is until Della Raye grew tired of eating the very same thing every morning. Though the menu never varied in the slightest, she made it to the breakfast table without fail. If she didn't she would get nothing, because there was never enough hoecake and gravy to go around.

After breakfast they had no more to eat until evening. At seven o'clock at night Cora served supper, and again the menu never varied—one slim bowl of black-eyed peas, and nothing else. As with breakfast, Della never got enough. In her first two months there, she lost forty pounds, dropping from a hundred and seventy-five to a hundred and thirty-four.

Della Raye brought few belongings from Partlow—a second dress, one change of underclothes, and her Bible. The same paper sack in which she had brought them now resided under her bed and served as her only storage space. She spent part of each day reading the Bible and praying. She no longer prayed for her free-dom; now she asked God to help her live through this freedom.

Besides starving, I thought I might freeze to death. There was no heat in the house at night, and they didn't have enough blankets to go around. I soon found out why the boys slept in their clothes; they did it to keep from freezing.

Della Raye washed her underwear and dresses several times a week, certainly more often than Cora was accustomed to, but she didn't seem to mind. Della bathed more often than the rest of them too, and using an ancient iron heated on the cookstove, she ironed her dresses.

The baby, as they referred to three-year-old Bonnie, worried Della. She had never seen a child so dirty. After fretting over the baby's condition for several days, she finally asked Cora if she could give Bonnie a bath. Cora said that would be fine, so Della heated the bath water the same way they normally did on Saturdays. She carried the washtub out into the yard, filled it with water, and built a fire under it. When the water was warm, she carried the tub inside, undressed Bonnie, and immersed her in it. The little girl was unaccustomed to taking baths, but she splashed water and enjoyed herself as Della scrubbed off layers of grime and dirt. She got quite a surprise while washing Bonnie's hair: she discovered it was blonde. Before the bath, Della had thought the baby's hair was brown or black.

When they finished the bath, Della sat and brushed Bonnie's hair. The baby loved the attention. During the brushing, Bonnie wrapped her arms around Della's neck, lay her head on her shoulder, and fell asleep.

Cora had saved some flowered feed sacks, and from one of these Della made Bonnie a little dress and a pair of panties, cutting them out with care and backstitching every seam. That evening the little girl delightedly paraded her new clothes before the family. Bonnie had found someone she needed, and so had Della Raye.

The boys may have been mischievous and ill-mannered, but having firsthand knowledge of how people become products of their environment, Della forgave them for their devilishness and got along with them reasonably well. One day two of the younger boys took her for a walk through the woods to show her their swimming hole. Having never been in the woods before, Della enjoyed hiking there and back. The swimming hole, a deep pool located at the bend of a heavily-wooded creek, made a pleasant setting compared to the rubble-strewn clearing around Richard's house.

A few days, later Richard came in from the field looking for the younger boys to help him with a chore. Although it was only seven in the morning, Cora told him they had already gone to the swimming hole. "I'll go get them," Della offered. "I know where the swimming hole is."

Della Raye was looking forward to the outing and set off into the woods alone. Fresh and sparkling with dew, the early morning forest was a busy place. She found herself walking through a fascinating world she had never known. Brilliant rays of sunshine danced in and out of the leafy canopy as she walked; birds chirped and flitted happily from branch to branch in the trees above, while furry creatures rustling in the leaves below drew her attention at every step.

No obvious path marked the way to the swimming hole, but she remembered finding it easily the day the boys had taken her there. The surrounding woods appeared familiar, and she recalled about how long it had taken them to get there the first time. She knew she would soon come to the creek, the swimming hole, and the boys.

She walked a while longer, and somehow it seemed to be taking too long. A tiny red flag went up in her mind, a disquieting whisper that something was wrong. But what could be wrong? How could one miss finding a creek and a swimming hole? The boys had to be close by. She decided to holler for them. As the sound of her voice echoed through the woods, she stood still and listened for their answer. None came. Maybe she hadn't hollered loud enough. She hollered louder. Still no answer.

She must have been wrong about the walking time. She went a little further, then stopped and yelled again. She choked as she yelled, and the alarm in her own voice surprised her. Was she alarmed? No, of course not. She'd find them soon.

Della walked on, and the woods became thicker, deeper, and totally unfamiliar. She yelled for the boys. No answer. She yelled again, and again, and again. She walked faster; maybe she ran.

Having spent her life inside a fenced compound, the immensity of the woods was inconceivable, the idea of being lost in them beyond her grasp. The forest became dark, engulfing—an alien place that had no end. Della Raye ran, screamed, and bawled like an animal. Her breath came in great gasps. She stumbled, fell, clawed her way back to her feet, and ran on. She could no longer hear the sounds of the forest, or her own screams. She left her awareness behind.

Sometime later, Della Raye found herself sitting under a tree, her throat scratchy and raw from screaming, her eyes red and puffy from crying. She looked down at herself. Dirt and mud streaked her torn dress; her arms and legs were a mass of bleeding scratches. Her bruised body felt sore in a half-hundred places, and she was too exhausted to stand. She didn't know where she was or how far she had run.

Della sat limply under the tree for what seemed a very long time; how long, she didn't know. Finally, she pulled herself to her feet, looked around wearily, and began walking to somewhere. She walked in a straight line, or so she thought, and never stopped.

At last, she heard a faint noise somewhere in the distance, the popping sound of a gasoline engine. She turned toward it, and as she walked the noise grew steadily louder. Suddenly, she walked out of the woods and found herself standing on a narrow dirt road.

The engine was coming closer. Della looked in the direction of the noise and saw a blur of yellow. She didn't realize until then that she'd still been crying. The noise turned out to be Richard, coming down the road on his old yellow tractor. She had been found, but she was too numb to feel happy. She simply stood and waited for him.

"Where you been, girl?" he said. "We been lookin' everywhere for you."

Della pointed back toward the woods.

"Were you lost?" he asked. She nodded. Richard shook his head. "You oughta be more careful about things like that. Don't you know not to go walkin' around in the woods if you don't know where you're goin'?"

"What time is it?" she asked.

"It's three-thirty in the afternoon," he said. She had been lost for more than eight hours. Della climbed onto the tractor, sunk to the floorboard, and rode to the house.

She may have been free, whatever that meant, but Della Raye felt more alone now than she could ever remember. The boys seemed to like her, but they were just boys, and there were too many of them anyway. Cora treated her decently, but she and Della would never be close.

She thought of Partlow often. At times she longed for it—for familiar faces, however strange some of them may have been; for familiar surroundings, however bleak they had been; for someone, anyone, who might understand or at least share her misery, for enough to eat.

But Della remembered her friend Maudie and others who had left Partlow and returned when the world outside overwhelmed them. She had never understood what it was that chased them back, and whatever it was frightened her terribly; but she had promised herself if she ever got the chance to change her life, she would not live it as her mother had lived hers. She vowed not to let the world defeat her, and every day and every night, she prayed for the strength to keep that vow.

All my life I had thought my troubles would be over if I ever got out of Partlow. I soon learned better than that.

A week or so after Della arrived at Richard's place, he handed her a letter. The return address read: Miss Delia Matthews, Partlow State School, Tuscaloosa, Alabama.

"Massie!" Della shrieked. "It's a letter from Massie!"

Massie had written her a long letter, asking about Richard's place, about his family, about how she was getting along, and sending greetings from some of her friends at Partlow. Hungry for news of the familiar and elated to hear from Massie, Della read and reread the letter. Massie also included some stamps, so Della wrote back and told her of the conditions at Richard's place. A short while later she received a package; Massie sent her several rolls of toilet paper and a sack of candy.

From then on Della received a package from Massie every week. The packages contained various essentials, but always toilet paper and candy. Because the boys seldom had a chance to even

taste candy, Della shared with them. One week Massie went over-
board; she sent her a full box of Almond Joys—twenty-four bars.
After the mail arrived, Richard handed Della the package and
went to sit in the porch swing. She opened it, took out two candy
bars, and put the rest under her bed. Then she walked out to the
porch and gave one to Richard. He smiled, thanked her, and they
sat and enjoyed them together.

The next morning, Della's candy bars were gone; even the
box was missing. She told Richard they had disappeared, and
that she felt sure the boys had taken them. He called each boy
in separately and quizzed him in front of Della, but they all
denied any knowledge of the candy. When he finished the
questioning, Richard looked at Della Raye and shrugged.

"Those boys are lying, Uncle Richard," Della said angrily.
"You know it as well as I do. You can see it in their faces."

Richard looked as though he might agree with her, but Cora
interrupted before he could answer. "I'll have you to know,
Della Raye, that my boys don't lie," Cora told her bluntly. "And
they don't steal either." Neither Della Raye nor Richard said
another word. After that Della carried her candy in her pockets
or hid it from the boys, and her days of sharing were over.

*I probably shouldn't have accused the boys directly that way, but I
didn't know any other way to handle it. Growing up as I had, I really
didn't know how to act in most situations.*

Richard was not only a sharecropper, but also an entrepre-
neur of sorts. He sold moonshine whiskey. For awhile Della
Raye was not aware that he owned a still, and she never did
learn its whereabouts. She knew he got drunk occasionally,
and wondered where he got his liquor, but in her naiveté, she
didn't realize he made it himself.

One Saturday morning, Richard asked her to go for a ride
with him on his old tractor, the only transportation he had. He
appeared in a good mood, and since in his strangely impersonal
way Richard seemed to like her, Della Raye assumed he had
asked her along because he enjoyed her company.

When Della stepped onto the tractor, she noticed a large burlap bag resting on the floorboard. "What's in that bag, Uncle Richard?" she asked.

"Oh, just some stuff I gotta take around to different folks," he answered.

"What kind of stuff?"

"Oh, stuff from the garden, things like that," he said. "We gotta take it around to some of the neighbors." Since Richard didn't have much of a garden, his answer seemed curious, but Della shrugged it off.

The old tractor rattled, banged, chugged, coughed, and spewed great clouds of black smoke, and for all its effort, it crept down the road barely faster than a person could walk. Della Raye didn't mind, though; she felt happy that Richard had invited her along, and she enjoyed the ride.

Richard stopped at a farmhouse, a rather prosperous one, reached into the burlap bag and withdrew a small paper sack. "You wait here," he said. "I'll just be a minute." He knocked on the door, grinned, removed his hat when a man answered it, and walked in. After a few minutes he emerged, turned, waved at the man, and climbed back on the tractor.

They visited several houses that morning, most of them nicer than Richard's, and each time, he repeated the same scenario. Della's curiosity grew, so while she sat waiting for him at some stranger's house, she opened the burlap bag and peered into one of the small sacks inside. It was not something from the garden; it was a Mason jar filled with clear liquid. Della Raye thought it looked like water.

She didn't tell Richard that she had peeked into his sacks, but later that evening, she asked Cora about the liquid in the jars. "Oh, Della Raye," Cora said, shaking her head and grinning slightly. "Don't you know what that is? It's corn whiskey—moonshine. Richard sells it to them people."

"Where does he get it?" Della asked.

"He makes it. Don't tell nobody, though. It's against the law."

"Against the law?" Della said naively.

"Yeah, it's against the law. And Richard could go to jail if they caught him at it. Worries me to death that they might catch him."

The following Saturday, Richard asked Della to go for another ride. "Where are we going?" she asked.

"Oh, we're gonna make some more deliveries," he said lightly.

"I'm not going with you," she said.

"Why not?"

"I know what you're doing, and you could get into a lot of trouble. Maybe I would too."

"Aw, nobody's gonna catch me," Richard said, "'specially not with you ridin' along. Nobody'll even get suspicious that way."

"I can't be doing things that are against the law," Della told him. "I just got out of Partlow, and I have to stay out of trouble. And besides that, it's a sin."

"Oh, Della Raye, it ain't no sin," Richard said impatiently. "I'm just tryin' to make a living. Come on and ride with me."

"No," she said. "You just want me along so you won't get in trouble. I'm not going to do it." And she didn't.

Richard and his family never attended church, but Cora knew that religion played an important role in Della Raye's life. One day she mentioned to Della that she had heard a tent revival was coming to Athens. "It's supposed to start next Sunday," Cora told her. "I think you'd enjoy it, but I don't know how you'd get to town."

Della vowed to attend the revival. That Saturday she bathed, washed and ironed the better of her two dresses, and laid out her Bible. Recalling the terror of being lost in the woods, she asked God to help her find the way. Sunday morning at breakfast she announced her plan to walk to town and attend the revival.

Richard reminded her that she hadn't been back to Athens since the day she had left Partlow. "Now, Della Raye, you can't walk clear to town by yourself," he cautioned. "Remember what happened out there in the woods?" Then he pointed at the four younger boys and said, "Y'all walk to town with Della this morning and see that she don't get lost."

After breakfast Della Raye set out for town, the four ragtag boys leading the way. They had all gotten clean overalls and a bath the day before, but the hair on each of their heads was an unruly mess, and none of them wore shirts or shoes.

She didn't know what time the service began, but she knew they had a long way to go. Carrying her Bible in the crook of her arm, Della Raye walked with a hard, determined stride and never stopped to take a break. The boys could have made it sooner, but because Della was unaccustomed to walking long distances, it took them nearly three hours to cover the nine miles.

She had no idea how to find the church with the tent beside it, but Athens was a small town and the problem solved itself. When Della Raye and the boys stopped on the sidewalk and looked up and down the deserted, Sunday morning street, somewhere in the distance she heard singing—gospel singing—the kind she'd learned to love at Partlow. Her heart pounded, a real church, with a real congregation—people singing, praying, and worshipping together.

Like a soldier grasping his weapon, Della Raye clutched her Bible and followed the joyous sound down the street, the entourage of ragamuffin boys following behind. Her step quickened when she saw the church with the high steeple and the white tent sitting on the lawn, but a half-block away, she stopped cold. Her elation turned to terror in an instant. She had never been inside a church, or a tent, or with a group of people she hadn't met. She began to shake with fear, and fought to hold back tears that wanted to flood the vision of the tent and save her the anguish of dealing with it. Her stomach drawn into a hard knot, a terrible compulsion to turn and run nearly overwhelmed her.

She may have been twenty-four years old, but Della Raye was a woman-child, alone in an alien world. She felt light-headed and thought she might faint, but her feet remained frozen in place. She did not retreat.

Her terror had erased the music, but as her fear abated slightly, the sound slowly returned to her ears. What a glorious sound it was. The people were singing, in God's house.

While the boys watched with curiosity, Della Raye took a furtive step, approached the tent fearfully, pulled open the flap, and forced herself inside. She found herself standing at the back of the congregation, the jumble of wide-eyed boys tumbling into the tent and trying to hide behind her. Every head turned to stare at them, and all were dressed in their Sunday best. She felt like a street urchin, hopelessly plain and poor, while everyone else looked rich.

Della ducked into a chair, motioned the boys to do the same, and tried to become invisible. And though she felt terribly uncomfortable during the service, she listened to every word, and after a while, she even picked up a hymn book and tentatively joined in the singing. Several members of the congregation went to the front to sing at different times, some solo and some in groups. Others stood up to give personal testimonials, often at the urging of the young minister, who had noticed Della when she first appeared in the tent door.

"Oh, Lord," she prayed each time the minister caught her eye. "Please don't let him say anything to me." She thanked God each time he didn't.

When the service ended, Della Raye and the boys fairly jumped from their seats and exited the tent. Soon they were back on the road heading out of town, and she was more than relieved to be gone. Thinking over the day as she walked, however, Della couldn't help feeling pleased with herself. She had done what she set out to do. She had gone to church.

The next morning, Della Raye and the four boys were up and on the road again. The boys were dirtier than yesterday, especially their grimy feet, but they didn't care. She still felt self-conscious and afraid during the service, but a little less than she had the day before. Again they jumped up and left without a word to anyone when the service ended; but before they had walked a mile, a car pulled up beside them and stopped. The young minister smiled at her from the driver's seat.

"Need a ride, young lady?" the minister asked.

Della surprised herself with her answer. "Well, yeah. I guess we could use a ride." He pushed open the door and she stepped in as the boys piled into the back seat like a pack of hounds.

"I'm Brother Handlin, pastor of the church in Athens," the minister said warmly, and started down the road.

"Hi," Della replied nervously.

After an uncomfortable pause, he asked, "And your name?"

"Oh, I'm . . . Della Raye," she said, stumbling over her words. "Della Raye Rogers."

The young man was so nice-looking, so neatly-dressed, and so bright. And he was a pastor, whatever that meant. Della felt terribly ill at ease, but his warm smile disarmed her. She plunged on. "I've been staying out here with my uncle, and I'm pleased to make your acquaintance, Brother Handlin."

"How far is it to your uncle's place?" he asked.

"Nine miles," she replied.

"I saw you in church yesterday," the minister said. "Did you walk all the way to town and then back home last night?"

"Yes sir, I did," Della said proudly. "And I walked back again this morning too."

With that, she grew more comfortable. Her talkative nature took over, and they chatted amiably the rest of the way to Richard's place. As Brother Handlin stopped the car, the gang of boys leaped out, slammed his rear doors and ran for the house.

"Are you going to walk to town again tomorrow morning?" he asked Della.

"Yes, I am," she said. "I plan to come every day of the revival."

The young man shook his head. "That's a lot of walking," he noted. "I tell you what, I can't come and get you in the mornings, but I can give you a ride home in the evenings when the services are over."

"Oh, thanks," Della gushed. "And listen, if there's anything I can do for you, anything at all, you just let me know."

The minister looked at her with a warm grin and appeared to understand something she did not. "You should be careful who you say things like that to, Della Raye" he advised her.

"No, I mean it," she repeated. "Anything I can do—you just let me know." With a wan smile and a slight shake of his head, he drove away.

I was so naive; I didn't even realize what I was saying to him. That minister probably wondered where I'd been all my life.

Della Raye and the four boys walked the nine miles to town every morning of the revival. The boys were a filthy, smelly mess by the end of the week, but Brother Handlin drove them home every evening as he had promised.

One day Cora heard a knock at the door, looked out, and saw a taxicab sitting in the yard. A well-dressed young man was standing stiffly on the step. His hair was blond, his eyes deep blue, and his face very serious. "Is Della Raye Rogers here?" he asked impatiently.

"Wait here," Cora told him. "I'll get her."

"Della Raye, there's a fella at the door askin' for you," she said. "He rode clear out here in a taxicab."

"A man!" Della asked with surprise. "What does he look like?"

"Well, he's about your age; he's dressed nice, like a city guy; and he's pretty good lookin'."

Della couldn't imagine who would be coming that far to see her. She opened the door and stepped outside. For a long moment the handsome young man looked at her closely, maybe a little fondly, then he spoke. "Hello, Della Raye."

He stood average in height, was clean, well-built, and neatly dressed; and something about his thin kind face focused Della's attention. She looked deeply into his eyes and said, "Homer?"

"Yes, it's Homer," he answered with a hint of a grin. "How are you, Della Raye?"

"My lord, Homer! This is quite a surprise," she said excitedly. "I sure never expected to see you."

"Surprise!" he answered, suddenly angry. "I had a God-awful time finding you. Why haven't you answered any of my letters?"

"Letters?" she replied blankly.

"Yes, letters. First I get you out of Partlow, then I write you letter after letter and you won't answer. I even tried sending you a registered letter once."

Della Raye frowned. "I never got any letters from you, Homer. Not a single one."

"I don't know how that could happen," he said sharply.

"And did you say you got me out of Partlow?" she asked.

"Yes. I told you I was going to get you out of there when I left. I was gone a long time, but I came back to Tuscaloosa, went to work, and hired a lawyer. His name was McCollum. Paid him six hundred dollars. Part of that money was supposed to help you get on your feet after you got out."

Della Raye ran it all through her mind, trying to make sense of what he had said. "I never saw any of your six hundred dollars, Homer," she told him. "I didn't know you hired that lawyer, and I swear I never got a single letter from you."

Homer shrugged and waved his hand in resignation. "Oh, that money's gone," he said, his anger receding. "But at least it got you out. And listen, if anybody has been holding back your mail from you, it's a federal offense."

Breaking from his stare, Della Raye looked him up and down. "Gosh, Homer, I haven't seen you in ten years, maybe more. You sure look good. Where do you live?"

"In Tuscaloosa. I've got a good job there. I've done a lot since I left Partlow—went off to the war, got some schooling, worked at different things."

His anger gone, Homer smiled and looked at her with the kind, confident eyes she remembered from childhood. "You look good too, Della Raye," he said warmly. "It looks like things are kind of rough around here for you, though.""Yeah," she said, glancing around at the squalor that was Richard's place. "I don't even get enough to eat. In ways it doesn't seem much better than Partlow."

"Why don't you come back to Tuscaloosa with me?" Homer asked her. "I'll help you get a place and see that you're all right. We can find you a job."

The invitation stunned her. Leaving Richard's place and going with Homer sounded terribly inviting, almost a dream, but she shook her head. "No. I can't go back there. When Dr. Partlow let me go he told me I could never come back to Tuscaloosa."

Homer's eyes flared. "He told you that?!"

"Yes, he did," she explained. "He said that was part of the deal. If they let me out, I could never live in Tuscaloosa again."

"He can't do that!" Homer said angrily. "He hasn't got that kind of power over you. He's just bluffing. You can live anywhere you want to. He doesn't want you coming back to Tuscaloosa and causing trouble for him—afraid people might find out there's nothing wrong with you."

"You're just like me," he continued. "I went into the army, got shipped overseas and everything. And there I was, a kid from a mental institution. I didn't let anybody know it, though. I still don't."

"It sounds wonderful, Homer, but I'm on probation for six months," Della said, her tone nearly a plea. "If I do anything I'm not supposed to, Uncle Richard can put me back in Partlow."

"I doubt he could get that done even if he wanted to, Della Raye. If you come back to Tuscaloosa with me I'll take good care of you. I never forgot you in all those years, you know."

Della Raye was nearly moved to tears. "I know you didn't forget me, Homer, and I'm so thankful for you coming back and getting me out. I've always said you were the finest person I ever knew. And I'm sorry about you losing your six hundred dollars."

"Don't worry about that," Homer said. He looked as if he might ask her again to leave with him, but then he thought better of it. With drooping shoulders and saddened eyes, he turned away. "I wish you all the best, Della Raye, and I hope I get to see you again someday." He stepped into the taxi, and was gone.

She watched the car fade into the distance, and felt terribly alone.

Della told Cora how she had grown up with Homer and about the letters that Homer said he had written. Della couldn't imagine why she hadn't received them. Cora looked away as she spoke, and grew strangely quiet. "What's the matter?" Della asked.

Cora looked at the floor and spoke haltingly. "Richard's been takin' your letters out before you could see them, Della Raye. Dr. Partlow told him not to let you have any mail except from that Matthews woman, the one you call Massie." Della clamped her jaws and said nothing.

After supper that evening, she confronted Richard. "Yeah, I kept out some of your letters, Della," he admitted, obviously embarrassed. "Dr. Partlow told me not to let you have them."

"That's against the law," she said evenly. "It's a federal offense."

"Dr. Partlow told me to do it. I was just followin' orders," he replied lamely.

"He shouldn't tell you to do something like that," she said. "It's illegal. Where are my letters, Uncle Richard?"

He looked at the floor. "I ain't got your letters, Della Raye; I burned them up. I won't keep any more from you, though." His promise didn't matter; Homer never wrote again.

Even before her release, Dr. Partlow had expressed concern about Della Raye living with Richard; indeed, he had forbidden it until forced by the habeas corpus. In his letter to the Athens County judge, he had voiced a hope that neighbors would look in on her occasionally to ensure her safety and well being; and he also asked Mrs. Woodruff to visit Della and monitor the living conditions at Richard's place. Should she find the environment unfavorable, Dr. Partlow told her, he recommended that she try and relocate Della with another family.

The welfare director did stop by to visit on occasion, and one day she asked Della Raye if she would take a job if one came available. Della told her she'd love to have a job of any kind.

Della Raye had been staying with Richard and Cora for three long months when a car pulled up one Wednesday afternoon. A middle-aged man knocked on the door and asked for her.

"My name's Appletree," the man said in a voice friendly and sincere, "Donald Appletree. I live up near Veto, just a few miles north of here. Mrs. Woodruff sent me. She said you might be looking for a job."

"What kind of job?" Della asked.

"Taking care of my parents," he said. "They're getting old. Dad's blind and Mom's an invalid. I have a Negro woman that comes once a week and does their laundry, but they need somebody to stay with them and take care of them around the clock now."

"I know how to take care of folks like that," Della said, "but I don't know much about cooking."

"Mrs. Woodruff thought you'd be good at taking care of them," he said. "And don't worry too much about the cooking; they'll eat about anything you fix for them."

"I sure would like to have a job," she said. "Would I be staying with them?"

"Yes, you would," the man replied. "I'll pay you five dollars a week. I'll buy whatever groceries you need, and you can eat as much as you like."

"Who's that in the car with you?" Della asked.

"That's my girlfriend. I asked her to ride over here with me, thought maybe you'd feel more comfortable with another woman along."

The job sounded inviting, especially the part about eating. "My uncle is out working in the field," Della said. "I'll have to go in the house and talk to my aunt about it."

"That's okay," he answered. "I'll wait out here."

She went inside and told Cora about the job that the man had offered her. Cora listened quietly, nodding her head occasionally as Della talked. When Della finished, she asked, "What do you think I should do, Aunt Cora?"

"Listen, Della Raye," Cora said. "I love you, but you know as well as I do that we ain't got room for you here. If I was you I'd take it."

"What do you suppose Uncle Richard will think?" Della asked.

"I wouldn't worry about what he thinks," Cora answered. "I'd just go on with that man and take the job."

"Okay, that's what I'm going to do."

Della quickly gathered up her belongings, packed them into her grocery bag, stepped into Mr. Appletree's car, and rode away.

The Appletrees lived in a small country house; it was old, like them, but not rundown like Richard's. Their house was clean, and it had electricity, and it felt warm and comfortable. And though Della Raye didn't have her own bedroom, sleeping on a cot in the living room was a pleasure after sharing a room with four rowdy boys. She had to walk down a little hill to the outhouse, but it came complete with toilet paper.

Mrs. Appletree was eighty-four and bedridden, her husband's adoration all she had left. It never wavered, though, and it was enough. "Uncle Bill," a few years younger than she, lovingly called his wife Tish. Uncle Bill had lost his sight, but not his spirit. Short, bent, and wizened but too feisty to accept assistance, the old man used a crooked stick for a cane. With the stick he could feel his way along the path and make it to the outhouse and back on his own.

Della fell in love with the old couple and took to her job like a doting mother. Within weeks she would have Mrs. Appletree up and walking around the house for the first time in years; and since Uncle Bill's only requirement was that she take good care of his beloved Tish, he and Della Raye jibed from the start.

Della Raye had grown up in a crowd. Inundated with incessant talking, babbling, and cursing, her childhood had been engulfed by too many people in too little space. Now she slept in a room by herself. Ecstasy. For the first time in her life, she knew privacy and peace. The quietness of the woods, the smell of the house— her first awareness of the true meaning of the word, *home.*

Caring for the old and infirm came as second nature to Della Raye, and because Donald let her make up the grocery list each week, she tried her hand at cooking various dishes. At times her experiments worked well, but as Uncle Bill and several housefuls of smoke would attest, some of her meals turned out to be less than tantalizing.

Della Raye arrived at the Appletrees on a Wednesday. Richard came to get her the following Sunday. Crossing the covered porch with heavy, unsteady feet, he knocked loudly and impatiently. Della stepped out, pulling the door shut behind her. Richard stood swaying on his feet, holding tightly to the rail for support, his breath reeking of moonshine.

"Whatta you think you're doin' over here, Della Raye?" he asked with a drunken leer.

"I live here, and I'm taking care of these people," she said. "It's my job."

"Job? This is your job?!" he asked, his voice heavy with sarcasm. "You makin' any money here? It can't be much."

"I'm making five dollars a week, Uncle Richard. It may not be much, but it's more than nothing, like I was making when I was staying with you."

"Five dollars a week," he sneered. "I guess that is a little more 'n nothin', but you can't stay here, Della Raye. I'm takin' you back to my place where you belong."

"I don't want to go back there. I like it here. Besides, you don't have room for me at your place."

"I can tell you who your daddy is, Della Raye," he said. "I'll take you and show him to you. He's a businessman, with a family. He's even a deacon in his church."

Della Raye didn't know if she believed him or not, and because she had long since crossed that bridge anyway, she didn't care. "I don't want to know who my father is," she said evenly. "I don't want to see him. And I'm not going back to your place either."

"Aw, Della, you gotta come back," he slurred, and for a moment appeared to lose his balance. He lurched forward, groping with outstretched arms, and wrapped them around Della's neck. For a moment she thought he had grabbed her to break his fall, then she felt his sour whiskey breath hot on her face. Horrified at the thought, she realized that Richard was trying to kiss her.

"Stop that!" Della shouted, jerking her head away and shoving him across the porch. "What in the world do you think you're doing, Uncle Richard?"

He caught his balance, smiled crookedly, and shrugged his shoulders.

"You ought to be ashamed of yourself," she said. "I'm your niece."

"Why should I be ashamed of myself?" he answered. "We don't really even know each other, Della Raye. You don't seem like a niece to me."

"You don't feel like kin to me either," she snapped. "But don't take that to mean I'm interested in you, because I'm not."

Richard raised his hands clumsily and started to speak again, but Della cut him off. Clenching her fists into tight balls, she leaned forward with a face of fury. "Maybe you're not ashamed of yourself, Uncle Richard, but I'm ashamed for you."

Richard reeled backward off the porch, stopped, pointed an outstretched arm and wagged a finger at her. "I'm givin' you one week, girl," he said. "Then I'm comin' back for you. And you'd better come with me too, or I'll send you back to Partlow. You're on six months probation, you know."

He turned and staggered away.

All that week, Della wondered if Richard would come back or even remember what he had said. True to his promise, however, he showed up again the following Sunday. He came sober this time, and he had not forgotten his ultimatum.

Della met him on the porch. Cocksure of himself, Richard

tilted his head jauntily and asked, "You ready to come back now?"

"No," she said. "I told you I would not go back to your place."

"If you don't, I'm gonna take you back to Partlow," he warned.

"Go ahead and take me back then," Della countered. "I know what you want with me, and it's not going to happen."

He stared at her, his lips tight, his cocky eyes gone puzzled. Della returned his gaze, and spoke slowly and evenly. "I am not going with you, Uncle Richard. And don't come over here bothering me any more."

She turned her back on him, walked into the house, and shut the door.

I'd thought about it a lot that week. Since the welfare lady had got me the job, I knew there was no way he could make me come back.

As neighboring houses were not far distant in the hilly, closely-spaced farming community where the Appletrees lived, Donald gave Della Raye a bell to ring in case of emergency. The noise would bring help from the nearest neighbors. What the Appletrees didn't realize was that growing up as she had, Della Raye knew little fear of anything or anybody. Uncle Bill discovered that fact one night when a prowler paid them a visit, and Della discovered what a spirited old man Uncle Bill really was.

The house stood quiet, the night pitch-black. While Mrs. Appletree had already retired to her bed, Della Raye and Uncle Bill were in the living room. Della sat reading. Uncle Bill just sat. From the corner of her eye, Della thought she caught a faint movement outside the window. When she looked up it was gone, if she had actually seen anything at all, that is. She dropped her head and fell back to reading, but a minute later she felt the same sensation again. This time she stood up and walked around the room, stopping and peering out each window into the darkness. She saw nothing.

Blind as he was, Uncle Bill sensed her movement and probably her uneasiness. "What's wrong?" he asked.

"Oh, nothing," she said, passing it off lightly. " I thought I saw something move past the window a while ago, but I guess I was wrong."

When Uncle Bill stood up from his chair and started feeling his way toward the bedroom, Della thought little of it. Moments later, a heavy bang jarred the front door. Then another bang resounded, and another, threatening to knock the door off its hinges. Someone or some thing was pounding it fiercely.

"Just a minute," Della said loudly. Jumping up from her chair, she unlatched the door and threw it wide open. The shadowy outline of a huge black man filled the doorway. He stood hunched forward, his eyes staring dead into hers, his face grim as granite.

"Hi," Della said blithely. "What can we do for you?"

The man stared silently, and stood still as stone.

Uncle Bill's voice cracked like thunder. "Who's there?" he shouted from the middle of the room.

"It's a big Nigra man," Della said over her shoulder. "He's big as a house."

"What's he want?" Uncle Bill demanded.

"I don't know," she answered. "He won't say anything. He's just standing there."

"Tell him to get the hell outta here!" Uncle Bill roared.

That got Della's attention. She turned her head quickly, and the sight of the old man jolted her. Bent with age, he leaned heavily on the stick with his left hand; in his right, he wielded a shotgun. His weather-worn face was a mask of ferocity; his sightless eyes commanded the room.

"I said get the hell outta here, you SUMBICH!" Uncle Bill yelled. "I'LL KILL YOU!" Waving the shotgun around the room like a madman, he pointed it at Della Raye, the intruder, the ceiling, and all points in between.

Whatever the mysterious man had in mind—good or bad—he wanted none of Uncle Bill. As the old man shouted and blindly waved the shotgun around the room, he turned and ran off into the darkness.

Della Raye felt her heart pumping like a racehorse, but not from fear of the prowler. "He's gone," she told Uncle Bill, keeping her voice steady and low. "You can put the gun down now."

The old man stood listening for sounds from outside a minute longer, then his ire began to settle. Standing the shotgun on its butt, he propped himself with one hand on the gun barrel and the other on the stick. Then like a lecturing parent, he admonished Della Raye, "You gotta be more careful, girl. You can't be openin' the door to just anybody out here, 'specially not at night. You're supposed to ring that bell. Somebody could come in here and hurt us bad."

She didn't think so.

Minnie, the black lady who came to do the laundry each week, helped Della Raye solve a dilemma. A large, stout woman, talkative and outgoing, Minnie struck up a friendship with Della the first day she came.

Della noted how quickly and efficiently the woman accomplished her work, and guessed that Minnie could teach her something she had long been wanting to learn. One day as the big woman was washing clothes, running them through the wringer, and hustling baskets back and forth from the clothesline to the house, Della Raye asked her, "Minnie, do you know how to cook?"

Minnie stopped, looked at her with merriment in her eyes, and laughed heartily. "Do I know how to cook!" she said. "Lord, I've been cookin' for a big mess of people longer 'n I can remember."

"Do you know how to cook lots of different things?" Della asked.

"I sure do," she said. "I can cook about anything a body can eat."

"Would you teach me how to cook? I don't know much about it."

"Sure," Minnie said. "Tell you what, each week we'll sit down and decide what you want to learn how to cook. Then you can have Mr. Donald get the groceries we need, and the next time I come I'll show you how to cook it."

And so Della Raye learned how to cook.

Della Raye answered a knock at the Appletrees' door one day, and found Cora standing on the porch. "What brings you here, Aunt Cora?" she asked with surprise.

Cora looked pitiful. She was distraught, and even more exhausted than usual. "It's Richard," she said. "He got arrested last night for moonshining. They put him in jail."

"I'm sorry," Della said. "When will he get out?"

"Maybe not for a long time," Cora said fearfully.

"What are you going to do?"

Cora shook her head and looked at her bare feet. "I don't know. Me and the kids can't get along without him. The man that owns the land will just put us out of the house. I don't know what'll happen to us."

With a plea in her sunken eyes, Cora looked up at Della. "We could get him out on bail if we had some money, but we ain't got any. Have you got some you could loan us, Della Raye?"

Della felt her stomach knotting. She got paid once a week, and had saved all the money she'd made, five dollars at a time. She kept it in a drawer, a neat little stash; sometimes she counted it just for fun.

Finally she asked. "How much do you need?"

"Fifty dollars," Cora said, avoiding her eyes.

"Fifty dollars?! That's about all the money I've got," Della said.

"Richard would pay you back as soon as he could, Della. We just gotta get him outta jail."

Della Raye walked to her room slowly, opened the drawer, and counted out the only fifty dollars she had ever owned. She looked at it for a long moment, gathered it up, and returned to the porch. "Here," she said, and handed it to Cora.

"Thanks so much, Della," Cora said. "Richard will pay you back real soon."

He never did.

CHAPTER NINE

Climbing the Mountain

In going from Partlow to Richard's place, Della Raye had simply exchanged one hell for another, but she found living with the Appletrees therapeutic. She was well-fed; she enjoyed taking care of the old couple, and her life had some semblance of structure and balance. And though the pay was next to nothing, she was earning her room and board as well; for the first time in her life she felt she was earning her keep. She loved that feeling of independence, of paying her own way.

Della's complacency was not to last. Three months after coming to the Appletrees, she received a letter from Bessie Waterman, the Partlow attendant who, along with her husband, had passed the notes back and forth between her and Homer many years before. Mrs. Waterman had heard of Della's situation and offered to send her a train ticket to Woodstock, Alabama, a small town between Birmingham and Tuscaloosa. There, Della Raye could live with her son and his family, and with help from them, she might find a job.

The prospect of going back to Tuscaloosa, or near it, intrigued her. The thought of living in proximity to Partlow held no dread, and somehow she would feel closer to familiar territory there and to people she knew. Della was practically broke after loaning Richard her fifty dollars, but she'd been broke all her life. The train ticket would get her to Woodstock, and then she'd have an opportunity to find a job. She decided to go.

Della hated to break the news to Uncle Bill and Tish, and when she did, they begged her to stay. When Mrs. Woodruff heard she was leaving, she came to the house and also tried to talk her out of it. Citing how much Della had done to enrich the Appletrees' lives, the welfare director offered to help her get a pay increase if she would stay on with the old couple.

"I do love Uncle Bill and Miss Tish," Della told her, "and they've been good to me. But I feel like this is a chance to get on with my life."

She asked Mrs. Woodruff about the probation and about Dr. Partlow's warning that she could never live in Tuscaloosa again. And though the woman badly wanted Della to stay, to her credit she answered her honestly. The probation period was nearly finished, she told her, and Richard had already forfeited any control he had over her life. And as for Dr. Partlow's telling her she could never return, Mrs. Woodruff brushed that off by pointing out that Della was not actually going back to Tuscaloosa anyway.

The train took her back through Birmingham and toward Tuscaloosa, the same route she had traveled twenty years earlier on her way to Partlow. That long-ago passage had been traumatic, as had the return trek with Richard only six months ago. On this trip she felt apprehensive about the challenges of building a new life, but the sky shone silvery blue and the hills and meadows a brilliant green; she found herself enjoying the scenery for the first time.

When Bud Waterman and his family met her at the train station, Della Raye was wearing one of the faded dresses she'd brought from Partlow and carrying the other in the worn grocery bag along with her Bible. With her hair hanging straight down and blocked off squarely from having cut it herself, she looked as if she might have never seen a town before.

"Hi, Della Raye," Bud said with a welcoming smile. "My mom and dad told us all about you." He was a short, amiable, good looking man, and Della liked him instantly. His wife

Irma's good looks complimented his, but her smile was plastic and her greeting lukewarm at best. Their children, Susie and Ted, aged nine and twelve, were nicely-dressed kids who knew their manners. They grinned shyly and said, "Hi, Della Raye." She liked them from the start.

Bud worked as a dispatcher for the railroad, a good living, and provided a spacious four-bedroom home for his family. He and Irma slept in the largest bedroom while Susie and Ted each occupied a smaller one. Della was left with a tiny room tucked away at the back of the house, but she didn't mind. The house had electricity, as did virtually all houses in the town, and now she could enjoy an indoor bathroom as well. And at last she had a bedroom of her own. The first time it rained, however, she awoke and discovered that the small size of the room was not it's worst failing. But Della Raye was used to far worse things than that; she just got up and moved her bed so that most of the dripping water missed it and fell on the floor.

Della cooked and cleaned the Waterman's house morning till night, and volunteered to do anything Irma could name. Irma welcomed the help and assigned her plenty of tasks to keep her busy, but during the day when Bud was at work and the children at school, she treated Della as if she were invisible, not even there.

Bud treated Della warmly, and the first Sunday after she arrived, he invited her to attend church with them. Feeling that she'd be out of place to accept the invitation, Della tried to decline. Bud knew she was religious and wouldn't hear of it. He insisted that she go, and from then on she accompanied them every Sunday. She loved going to church with the family, meeting people, and learning to mix with the congregation. Irma didn't share her joy.

Regardless of how their mother treated Della, Susie and Ted were unabashedly fond of the young woman who had moved into their house. Twice each week, on Sunday and Wednesday night, the children walked with her to attend prayer meetings at the church. Since Della Raye had never really had the freedom to be a child, she greatly enjoyed their company. And facing a new world that she knew little of, she felt like a child herself in many ways.

Bud's parents came to visit every other Sunday. With Woodstock being only a twenty-five mile drive from Partlow, Bessie and Ralph Waterman would arrive in time to go to church with the family on Sunday morning and then spend the rest of the day there.

A tall, thin, crippled man, Ralph had lost partial control of his left side in a stroke. His spirit had not been crippled, though, nor had his humanity. In his job as a Partlow attendant, he showed respect for all patients, regardless of their physical or mental condition.

Bessie Waterman treated Della decently and tried to include her in family conversations, but Ralph was the one who seemed truly fond of her. Knowing that Della Raye had no money, Ralph would take her aside each time they visited and say, "I know you don't have any money for personal things," and slip a dollar or two in her hand. She was too naive to realize he was sneaking it to her.

One Sunday Bessie walked into the room as Ralph was handing Della Raye a bill. He snatched his hand back, but not before Bessie saw him. "What are you doing?" the woman snapped. "Giving her money?!" Ralph looked at the floor sheepishly and said nothing. "We haven't got money for her," Bessie said. Then she pointed a finger at her husband and admonished, "Don't let that happen again."

It didn't happen again.

Della Raye felt embarrassed over the incident, as well as hurt and confused. Bessie Waterman had always seemed such a sweet person. She had cared enough to write her and send her a train ticket, yet in spite of all the work Della had done at her son's house, the woman begrudged her a few dollars. And though Bessie had promised they would help her find work in Woodstock, after she arrived she never heard another word of it. She had no idea how to go about finding a job on her own; the prospect of even attempting it filled her with terror.

They were nice to me, but I don't think they ever intended to get me a job. They just wanted me to do their dirty work for them.

After staying at the Watermans for two months, Della Raye began to feel more and more unwelcome, but she had nowhere else to go. Massie still worked at Partlow but now had an apartment of her own in Tuscaloosa. She wouldn't invite Della to live with her because of Dr. Partlow's warning that she could never return to Tuscaloosa.

While puzzling over the dilemma, Della Raye received an unexpected opportunity, or at least it appeared so at the time.

In a surprise visit one Sunday afternoon, Partlow's Naziesque personnel manager, Edna Coen, showed up at the Watermans. Accompanied by her sister, Judy, Edna marched in, introduced herself, and spoke to Della Raye in a warmer tone than she had ever heard come out of the stern woman's mouth.

Neither of the Coen sisters had ever married, but beyond that single similarity they were far different women. Edna possessed a cold intelligence that showed in her dark, ruthless eyes. Dr. Partlow had recognized in her an aptitude for handling the hiring and firing efficiently, and sent her to school to learn the job. Edna's stocky body bordered on being fat, and a close look at her taut face revealed a maze of jagged scars from a childhood accident. Some of the crisscross stitch marks remained, but as middle age approached the scars were losing their prominence and blending into a pale network that added to her severity.

Judy was attractive, and her sister's opposite: a slender, pleasant woman with a prim look that reflected a great deal of self pride. Judy also possessed intelligence, but she directed hers toward helping manage the Tuscaloosa paper mill instead of controlling other's lives, as Edna delighted in doing.

Judy and Edna lived with their aging parents in a spacious house in Cottondale, a small community on the northern outskirts of Tuscaloosa. Life could have been pleasant in such a home; unfortunately, Edna ran the show.

But that Sunday evening at the Waterman's house, Edna seemed sweeter than Della could ever remember. After a bit of small talk, she leaned forward with a concerned brow and asked, "Della Raye, I'll bet you'd like to have a job, wouldn't you?"

"Yes, I would," Della answered quickly. "That's why I wanted to come back from up north, so I could find a job."

"We live just north of Tuscaloosa," Edna said. "If you'd like to come and stay at our house we could help you find a job. It would be easier to find one there than here in Woodstock." Judy nodded her agreement.

Della Raye could not understand Edna being so helpful. But there was a lot she didn't understand. Maybe Partlow people acted differently when they were away from there. She liked the idea of leaving Woodstock, and the look on Irma Waterman's face said she liked it too.

"Our mom and dad are getting old," Edna continued, "and you can help out around the house till you get a job. We won't charge you any rent."

Della Raye looked around the room. Everyone seemed in agreement except the children, Susie and Ted. She smiled fondly and said, "I'm going to miss you guys."

"We're going to miss you too, Della," they replied tearfully.

Again Della Raye packed her grocery bag. She said good-bye to the Watermans, hugged the children, and stepped into the back seat of Edna's car.

The Coen sisters' parents, Dewey and Miss Myrtle, lived in a beautiful two-story home with four bedrooms—one on the first floor and three upstairs. The old couple lived downstairs, while Edna and Judy each occupied an upstairs room. The fourth bedroom was used for storage, and remained so after Della's arrival. She slept on a makeshift cot in Judy's room.

Dewey and Miss Myrtle welcomed her warmly. They were both pleasant people but they were old and had little to say about the running of the house. Edna outlined Della's duties, and though they sounded a bit excessive, she reminded herself that she was staying there rent-free. Without a word of protest, she plunged in.

Although the house had a modern bathroom, the Coens clung to the old habit of keeping slop jars under their beds for toilet use during the night. Della's first duty each morning was to gather up all the slop jars, carry them to the toilet, empty them out, and clean them. She also cleaned and dusted the entire house daily, and each week did the laundry and changed all the beds.

Edna quickly reverted to her old self—no more smiling, talking sweetly, or feigning compassion. She'd come home from work in the evening, plop down in a chair, and begin shouting orders. "Bring me something to read, Della Raye," she'd holler. "Anything but the Bible."

Unlike her sister, Judy treated Della decently, occasionally complimenting her on how well she took care of the house and her parents. And at that point in her life Della Raye was highly receptive to such praise.

Edna just used me, but Judy was nice. She meant well, and I just couldn't do enough for anybody who showed me a little compassion and love.

One Sunday morning Della Raye began to feel nauseous. She worsened through the day and by evening had body cramps, a high fever, and could hardly stand on her feet. She obviously needed medical attention, but no one offered to help. Finally at her father's insistence, Edna phoned a doctor late that evening.

Doctor Darden arrived at nine o'clock that night, checked Della over quickly, and said, "This girls needs to go to the hospital."

"We can't be responsible for putting her in the hospital," Edna told him. "She's one of those girls from out at Partlow. She's got no job, no money, and no insurance of any kind."

Doctor Darden exploded. "I don't give a damn what she doesn't have!" he roared at Edna. "You're going to be calling me again by midnight or one o'clock this morning, and she'll end up in the hospital if the ambulance has to come and get her."

The doctor was right. Later that night they called him again and he sent an ambulance for her. Della Raye had a serious infection, though its exact location was never clear. Dr. Darden treated her in the hospital for a week and never charged her a cent.

Edna, however, was distraught over her own potential liability. She went door to door soliciting money to pay for Della's hospital bill. Describing her as a pathetic case whom she was trying to help, Edna explained that Della was one of those "Partlow girls" who had nothing.

She went all over the neighborhood telling that. It was terribly embarrassing.

A few weeks later Della contracted a serious infection in a wisdom tooth, and again could get no one's attention until she passed out on the Coen's living room floor. Edna and Judy knew that Massie was off work that week, so the next morning they dropped Della off at her place and told Massie they didn't have time to take care of her. Massie's brother drove Della to a dentist, waited while he pulled her tooth, then returned her to the Coen's house so she could empty the slop jars and resume her daily chores.

Just as she had experienced at the Watermans, after she arrived at the Coens, Della Raye heard no more about anyone helping her find a job. But one day she got lucky. Judy and Edna's Aunt Bertha, a big friendly woman with a kind heart, stopped by for a visit. While there she asked Della what kind of work she had done at Partlow. When Della told her about the beauty shop, it caught the woman's attention.

"I've got a friend you need to talk to," Aunt Bertha said. "Myrta Poe. She owns Poe's Beauty Shop in Tuscaloosa. I could find out if she's interested in talking to you about a job if you'd like me to, Della Raye."

"Sure!" Della said excitedly. "I'd love that!"

Aunt Bertha and her husband returned the following

Sunday. "Mrs. Poe told me she'd like to talk to you, Della Raye. I can set it up for you any day this week," she said.

"I'll go anytime," Della answered, "but I don't know how to get there."

"I can tell you how to get there from here on a bus," Aunt Bertha said, but her husband interrupted.

"Bertha, this girl doesn't know how to ride buses," he said. "She's never done anything like that. We're going to come and get her and drive her to Mrs. Poe's."

Like many beauty shops of that era, Myrta Poe's shop adjoined her house. Modern, decorative, and well-equipped, it was large enough to employ several full-time beauticians. A successful businesswoman with an electric personality, Myrta Poe, an energetic widow with devil-may-care eyes, stood tall and trim. Sixtyish, thin-faced and stylishly pretty, the feisty woman dressed well, wore the proper makeup, knew how to laugh, and challenged the world on her own terms.

Myrta Poe knew about Della's background in Partlow, but she believed that everyone deserved a chance to prove themselves. Her first look at Della Raye appeared to test that belief, however.

Having never been inside a beauty shop other than the small one at Partlow, Della felt frightened and intimidated following Aunt Bertha through the door of Poe's. And she wanted to turn and run when the woman announced loudly without breaking stride, "Myrta, this here's Della Raye!"

Myrta Poe whirled around and flashed a welcoming smile, which soon began to fade at the sight of Della's stringy hair, colorless dress, and total lack of makeup. Myrta quickly regained her smile, however, and held out her hand and said, "Hello, Della Raye."

"Hello, Mrs. Poe," she answered as calmly as she could. Myrta saw that the girl was utterly without manners or social acumen, but she appreciated Della's straightforward politeness. For a long, uncomfortable moment the tall woman looked her up and down; then she frowned, looked her dead in the eye, and said, "Don't you think you ought to try and find a job in a restaurant or something like that, girl?"

"No," Della answered. "I don't know anything about restaurant work."

"What makes you think you can do beauty work?"

"I've fixed hair for a long time," Della Raye said. "It's all I know how to do. I'm good at it too," she added, hoping she sounded more confident than she felt.

Myrta Poe saw through Della's bravado, but she loved it. "I can try you for a while," she said. "We'll start you on an apprenticeship, and see how that works out. You'll be an apprentice for six months, if you make it that long, and you won't draw any pay until you finish it."

"That's okay," Della said, beaming all over. "I can do it."

"All right," Myrta answered. "But we're going to have to cut that hair and fix you up a little before you start meeting customers."

Before she would allow her to start on regular customers, Mrs. Poe wanted to see some of Della's work. The following Monday when she started work, Bessie Waterman came in and had Della give her a permanent. Myrta looked over the job critically but said nothing. The following day Massie came in for a shampoo and wave. Again Myrta didn't comment, but the following day she directed a customer to Della Raye to have her eyebrows arched and dyed.

As Della continued to demonstrate her abilities, her lack of manners didn't seem to bother the customers at all. She talked more than her share, but she entertained them in the process, and her natural charm easily made up for her backward ways. Myrta could see that everyone liked her.

At the end of the first week Myrta Poe opened the cash register and looked at Della. "I'm not going to let work of that quality go out of here without paying you, Della Raye," she said. And though technically she didn't owe Della Raye a thing, that Friday evening Mrs. Poe paid her four and a half dollars.

I had never been so proud. I would have framed that four and a half dollars if I hadn't needed it so badly.

Myrta Poe gave Della Raye her own chair in the shop and a regular wage after her first week. Edna Coen was happy that Della got the job; now she could charge her twenty-five dollars a month for rent and still require all the household chores as well.

Each morning Della Raye got up early enough to empty and clean the slop jars before leaving for work. In the past Judy had always dropped Edna off at Partlow on her way to the paper mill, then picked her up again in the evening. Now, rather than drive a few miles out of their way, the sisters dropped Della off at a bus stop where she caught a bus on to her job. Then in the evening, she had to leave work early in order to catch the bus back to the same stop to meet them on the way home.

Myrta Poe gave her Wednesday afternoons off; that's when Della did the laundry, cleaned the house, and changed the beds. She did get a slight break on weekends; Massie's brother would pick her up after work on Saturday and take her to stay at Massie's apartment until Sunday evening.

And to Della's surprise, Homer showed up again. He heard that she had moved back to the area and phoned her at Massie's apartment. They began dating on Saturday nights— going out to movies, to restaurants, and taking long walks together. They talked at length of their childhood experiences in Partlow and the problems of adjusting to the outside world. Since Della had only Massie with whom she could discuss such things and Homer had no one, these conversations were therapeutic for both of them.

Della Raye knew little of the opposite sex, and her mother's experience had made her leery of men in general. She felt that men had helped ruin Ruby's life, and she determined not to let them ruin hers. Homer was different, however. She trusted him, and spending time with him seemed more like visiting with an old friend than like dating.

As they walked closely together along darkened, tree-lined sidewalks, Homer was always the perfect gentleman. And unlike most dating couples, they seldom touched. Only once did Homer venture a kiss, and that was simply a fleeting peck on the lips as he left her at Massie's doorstep. She felt totally at ease in his company and didn't know why neither of them felt compelled to act more intimately. She didn't question their relationship. It felt natural the way it was.

The people at Partlow knew that Della Raye had returned to the area and had taken a job in Tuscaloosa. One weekend as a group of guests were touring the institution, one of them commented on Partlow's beauty shop. Massie, who was working nearby, overheard the guide tell the guests that a girl who used to work there now lived off the grounds and was attempting to make it in a regular shop. The girl had some real problems, though, the guide explained; she couldn't even get around town by herself—she had to be carried back and forth to work by normal people.

The disparaging comments—obviously meant to imply that Della Raye was feebleminded and inept—hurt Massie deeply. They hurt Della too when Massie told her what she had overheard, but she had no recourse except to grit her teeth stubbornly and go on. Myrta Poe noticed that Della seemed unusually quiet at work and asked if something was bothering her. When Della told Myrta what the Partlow employee had said, the lady's jaws clamped shut and her eyes blazed.

"You and I are going shopping, girl," Myrta said. "And after that we're going to pay a visit to Partlow."

Myrta Poe took Della Raye to the finest dress shop in Tuscaloosa and outfitted her colorfully and grandly. Then she styled Della's hair, applied professional touches of makeup, and escorted her to Partlow to visit her mother.

Ruby was proud to see Della Raye looking so prosperous and to hear Myrta Poe bragging about her daughter's accomplishments, but Myrta didn't stop there. She took Della to the

Administration Building, where Edna Coen scowled when she asked to see Dr. Partlow.

Obviously taken aback at Della's appearance as he walked out of his office, Dr. Partlow stopped short and exclaimed, "Why, hello, Della Raye."

"Hello, Dr. Partlow," Della answered, and before she could say another word her tall chaperone introduced herself.

"Dr. Partlow," the stunning woman said. "I am Myrta Poe, proprietor of Poe's Beauty Shop here in Tuscaloosa. I know you're all interested in Della's well being, and I just wanted you to know how well she's doing. She has her own chair in my shop; she learns fast, and is the best apprentice I've ever had. Della Raye is just an excellent beautician, and so smart!"

"Well, thank you, Mrs. Poe," Dr. Partlow replied hesitantly. "I'm glad to hear she's doing so well." Then he turned to Della and said; "You be careful, Della Raye. It's a big world out there; you need to take care of yourself."

The news of Della Raye's visit traveled quickly around the asylum. Shortly thereafter someone at Partlow commented that if Della wasn't careful, she could get herself into trouble with men, because there was only one way she could be making that much money. When she and Myrta Poe heard that outrageous accusation, they laughed out loud.

Myrta Poe did much to show Della Raye the ways of the world, eventually taking her on a vacation through the American West where they visited relatives of Poe's, national parks, and Indian reservations. Although in her core Della Raye was a kinder and less vindictive person than Myrta Poe, they were kindred spirits. The feisty lady appeared at a crucial time in her life and encouraged her to reach for the top rung.

Homer didn't touch her when it happened, he didn't even take her hand, but one night as they walked along side by side, he suddenly said, "I love you, Della Raye, and I want to marry you."

She stopped short, and for a long moment they stood in shadowy silence. "I can't marry you, Homer," she said quietly.

"Why not?" he asked, his voice choking.

"You're the finest man I've ever known, Homer, but you're just a good friend to me. I don't feel like I love you."

"I've always loved you, Della Raye," he said. "You could learn to love me."

"Oh, Homer. I just don't know."

"Just think about it, please."

Paying rent at the Coen's as well as doing all the work seemed excessive, but they had taken her in before she had a job, so Della didn't complain. Then she got a raise. It amounted to only a few dollars a week, but it was the first pay raise she had ever received.

Edna saw newfound wealth in Della's raise. Now she could raise her rent. Edna didn't approach Della directly; she recruited Judy, and together they tried to talk their parents into confronting Della about increasing the rent. The idea backfired. Instead of taking up their cause, Dewey and Miss Myrtle shamed them for even considering such an idea after working the girl the way they had.

Edna didn't give up easily. Knowing Massie's passive nature, she pressured her to approach Della about paying more rent. The Coens did live in Cottondale, and because Massie still feared Dr. Partlow's order that Della Raye was not to live in Tuscaloosa, she went along with Edna's request.

The first time Massie broached the subject of the rent, Della told her she didn't feel she owed them any more, especially with all the extra work they made her do in their house. The next time she mentioned it, Della looked at her suspiciously. "Massie, did Edna put you up to this?" she asked. "Do they want to go up on my room and board?" Massie didn't answer.

"That's what I thought," Della said. "So they want me to pay more rent."

"Don't you think you could afford to pay them a little more now?" Massie asked.

"I pay them twenty-five dollars a month, and I do all the

washing, vacuuming, dusting, and I change the beds and empty their stinking slop jars," Della said. "How much more is a little more?!"

"But this way you have a place to stay," Massie reasoned, "and it's in Cottondale."

"I don't care," Della said. "If that's what they want I'll just find another place to stay, maybe in Tuscaloosa where I'll be closer to work."

"You know Dr. Partlow said you weren't ever supposed to live in Tuscaloosa again," Massie reminded her.

"Dr. Partlow, Dr. Partlow, Dr. Partlow. That's all I've heard all my life," Della said. Her eyes flashed with the defiance that had carried her through twenty years of hell. "He's not going to run my life forever."

"You could get into a lot of trouble, Della Raye," Massie cautioned.

"I've been in trouble before," she said.

Della called Anna Lee Dockery. The pretty young woman who had secretly treated her head wound years before no longer worked at Partlow. She lived in a small house in Tuscaloosa now, along with her husband and little boy. They really had no extra room, but Anna Lee didn't hesitate when Della called. She was welcome to come and live with them.

After her husband returned from the war, Anna Lee had quit work to start a family. She was still her petite, attractive self after giving birth to a child; and her husband, Vernon, was thin, good looking, and as kind as her. They lived near downtown Tuscaloosa too, only a quarter of a mile from Myrta Poe's shop.

Edna was livid when she heard that Della planned to leave, but Della didn't care. She didn't explain why she was leaving nor did she make a scene; she simply thanked the Coens and left.

Anna Lee and Vernon drove to Cottondale, helped Della Raye with her bags, and brought her to their home. She had a few more belongings now, and had finally worn out her old paper sack. On the way to their house, Della explained the situation at the Coens, and insisted on paying them rent. "I don't mind paying," she said. "I'm just tired of being treated that way."

"All right," Anna Lee told her, "but I won't take a bit more than thirty-five dollars a month. And you won't have to have do all the cleaning and dusting at my house. That's my job."

Their home may have been small, but it was bright, sunny, and filled with love. In the six months that Della Raye would stay with Anna Lee and Vernon, she would never hear an unkind word pass between them. Their laughing little boy reflected his parent's affection for him and for each other. Della spoiled him like a doting aunt.

The arrangement of the Dockery's little house required Della to walk through their bedroom in order to reach the bathroom, but they never said a word. Anna Lee washed and ironed her clothes, changed her bed, cooked her breakfast every morning before she went to work, and packed her a lunch. And though the shop was only three blocks from the department store where Vernon worked, he dropped Della off at Myrta Poe's door each morning and then picked her up again in the evening.

I felt like a queen. I didn't know people could be so nice.

Homer was determined to marry Della Raye. "I love you, Della," he repeated often. "And I know you could learn to love me."

"No, Homer," she told him. "I appreciate everything you've done for me and I think the world of you, but I don't love you."

Homer persisted, and Della felt a terrible obligation. He had come back after ten years and kept a promise that she had forgotten. He had worked hard, saved a staggering amount of money, hired a lawyer, and set her free. And he loved her.

Early in 1950, she reluctantly agreed. "All right, Homer," she told him one evening. "I'll marry you in September."

Homer's face lit up like that of a small child's. From that moment on, he talked of nothing but September.

I don't really know why I said September, except that it gave me a chance to put it off a while longer.

Homer didn't care when; he would have married her anytime. As the months rolled by, Della became more and more uneasy. She didn't know if she could really go through with it, and she had never seen Homer so happy.

As Della's feelings of guilt and obligation propelled her toward an unwanted marriage, fate intervened. The Korean War began. Only five years after the end of World War II, the United States found itself involved in another fight. With Homer's combat experience placing him at the top of the list, he was drafted into the military a second time, and ordered to report in August.

He phoned her immediately. "I've been called back in, Della Raye," he said, desperation in his voice. "We'll have to get married before September, even before August."

She held back. With their lives changing so rapidly, Della told him she needed time to think. But with the deadline quickly closing in, Homer continued to press her. Finally she told him firmly, "No. I said I'd marry you in September, and I won't do it before then."

"But I won't even be here in September," he pleaded. She didn't answer.

Della walked Homer to the bus station the morning he left. She had never seen such pain in his eyes, and had never felt such guilt for having caused it. The single kiss they had shared months before would remain their only one. After a strained goodbye she watched him ride away. He never looked back.

One week later Della received a letter. "I knew what you had been through," Homer wrote, "and I wanted to marry you before I left so you could have my paychecks to live on while I was gone. But I don't think you ever intended to marry me anyway, because you don't love me. I will never see you again. Homer."

Tears of sorrow and relief flooded her eyes as she read. Life had always been hard; why did it have to be so complicated as well? She gripped the letter tightly and asked God to keep Homer safe.

Homer returned to foreign shores to fight in another war. He would always be her hero, in many ways.

Myrta Poe had won all the battles she chose to fight and saved enough money to retire. When she decided to close her shop, she suggested that Della Raye call the owner of Amy's Beauty Shop and inquire about a job there. Amy had trained under Mrs. Poe and respected her judgment as far as Della's talents were concerned, but she felt uneasy about her background. At Della's suggestion, Amy talked with Maggie Williams; Maggie gave her a fine recommendation, but still Amy wasn't satisfied. She called Partlow's main office to inquire further. Someone there blackballed Della—spoke disparagingly of her character and fueled Amy's uncertainty. Amy told Della she didn't have a place for her in her shop.

Because Missy Horton was known to frequent dance halls and bars, Horton's Beauty Shop had been the last on Della's list. After Amy turned her down, however, she had no choice but to call Missy. Missy listened to Myrta Poe's glowing recommendation and promptly hired her. The other beauticians in Missy's shop wore too much makeup and tended to be the same wild caliber as their boss, but though Della Raye disagreed with their lifestyle and never uttered a single curse word, they liked her gregarious ways. The job seemed to be working well.

A few weeks after Della went to work at Horton's, Missy took her aside and told her that she had decided to handle all the cash transactions herself. Della Raye and the other women who worked there were not to enter the cash register. Della saw no problem with the customers paying Missy directly, but a few days later she noticed the other beauticians again making their own change. Being new to the shop, she shrugged it off and continued to tell her customers to pay Missy.

Unbeknown to Della, the money in the register had come up short on several occasions. When Missy confronted the other employees, one of them had accused the new girl. "It must be Della Raye," the woman said to Missy and the others. "You know she's never had any education; she probably can't even count money."

"I'll take care of that," Missy replied, and that's when she told Della to stop using the cash register.

Then Missy went to a dance with some friends and learned the truth. After several drinks one of her friends started bragging that Irma, a beautician at Missy's shop, had given her a permanent at no charge. And Missy soon learned that she was not the only customer to receive such treatment. Evidently, the naive Irma had thought she could garner favor by treating her boss's friends to free hairdos.

Missy confronted a contrite Irma and told her to stop the free service. She then explained the mystery of the missing money to the other employees but told them not to mention it to Della. She'd rather leave things the same and not have to explain her actions to Della Raye.

It became obvious that Della was the only employee not allowed to operate the cash register, and she remained unaware of all that had transpired behind her back. Then one day another beautician got mad at Irma and decided to get even. The woman took Della Raye out to dinner and told her the whole story.

A dinner invitation from an overly-painted beautician, who frequented bars and seldom spoke to her, surprised Della more than a little. She kept her side of the conversation light that evening and waited to find out what the woman had on her mind. When the beautician began to tell her the story behind her banishment from the cash register, Della listened quietly.

When the beautician finished her story, Della Raye looked at her with a resolve that took her by surprise. "If that's all Missy thinks of me," Della said, "then I'm not going to work there any more. I don't want to work with any of those girls after they've done me like that."

"Oh, Della Raye," the woman said. "Don't let anybody know I told you this." Della didn't promise her anything; she'd been part of the conspiracy too.

The following morning, Della told Missy she was leaving and why. Missy was shocked. "Oh, Della Raye, please don't leave," she pleaded. "It wasn't your fault."

Della Raye stood on principle. "No, it wasn't my fault," she said. "But you let me take the blame for somebody else's stealing without me even knowing it, while everybody else knew the truth. You automatically blamed me and wouldn't trust me to run the cash register like the others. And after you found the guilty person you still treated me like a thief."

"I'm so sorry all this happened," Missy said, nearly in tears. "You're one of my best operators, Della Raye. Please stay."

"No," Della said. "I won't work for you after you've treated me this way." She gathered up her personal belongings and walked out of Missy's shop.

Myrta Poe was livid when she heard the story. For a while she stomped around her house and vented her rage; then after regaining a bit of self control, she picked up the phone and dialed Amy.

"Amy, this is Myrta Poe," she fumed. "You ought to be ashamed of yourself, girl. When you got cold feet about hiring Della she had to go over and work for Missy Horton. Well, you know how Missy is; she treated her like a dog and tried to take advantage of her. But Della Raye is better than all that. She quit Missy today."

"Oh, Mrs. Poe," Amy replied with true concern. "I didn't mean to cause trouble for the girl."

"Della Raye is a jewel," Myrta Poe said. "Nothing but a jewel."

Della went to work for Amy the following week.

CHAPTER TEN

Holding Her Own

For whatever reasons, we humans tend to fashion both our heroes and the loves of our lives in our own minds before they come along; and when they appear we often find them surprisingly different than we had imagined. Floyd Hughes seemed an unlikely match for Della Raye, but considering her background, perhaps anyone would have.

She hadn't felt like dating for several months after Homer left, but eventually started seeing a young man named Fred, whom she had met while living with the Coens. A regular guy and a rather unexciting fellow, Fred worked at the rubber plant. He was polite and considerate, and because they both enjoyed gospel songs and movies, they went out regularly on weekends. Like Homer, Fred seemed nothing more than a friend to Della Raye. And also like Homer, he had more romantic notions toward her.

Massie was forty now, and though she had known romance early in her life, she had never married. Twenty years before, she had loved a man with the unlikely name of Gewin Thigpen, but Gewin had broken up with her and married another woman. Massie would never love another; however, so she remained single. Then Gewin's wife died and he and Massie found each other again. They were dating now, and eventually would marry after all.

Fred and Della Raye sometimes double-dated with Gewin and Massie, and one weekend the four of them had planned to drive to Nashville to attend the Grand Ole Opry. Early in the week, however, Fred learned that he was scheduled to work the coming weekend and wouldn't be able to go. Gewin told Della Raye that a good friend of his might like to go along and be her date. His friend was several years older than her, Gewin explained, but he depicted him as sensible, gentlemanly, and fun. She told Gewin she'd like to meet his friend.

Della Raye describes her first impression of Floyd Hughes in two words: handsome and nice. Stout, erect, near six feet tall with a wide face, square-set jaw, and strong features, Floyd faced the world with a serious countenance but knew how to smile. The gray eyes brooked no nonsense, but they could laugh too. He turned out to be more than a little older than her—seventeen years to be exact—but a shock of dark, wavy hair atop a high forehead lent him an irresistible flare of boyish handsomeness.

Floyd's straightforward manner, disarmingly direct, let everyone know where they stood, like it or not. Della Raye admired that in him, as well as his strength and honesty. She and Floyd decided to go to Nashville with Gewin and Massie that weekend.

Della Raye had met few people as plain-speaking as Floyd, and he proved to be nearly as talkative as she. Riding in the back seat of Gewin's car, she laughed and joked and learned much about Floyd on the way to Nashville. He was a skilled machinist who made a good living, but the rest of what she learned would have scared off most young women. Della Raye had weathered more in her short life than most people ever do, and she feared little. Besides, she loved talking with him.

Floyd hid nothing from her. He was a widower whose first wife had died two and a half years before and left him with five daughters. His two oldest daughters were married and one of them had two small children, making Floyd a grandfather at forty-four. Of the three younger daughters who still lived at home, the oldest was an invalid. Now sixteen, the girl had suffered from crippling rheumatoid arthritis since the age of five.

The four of them stayed at a motel that night, Della Raye and Massie in one room and Floyd and Gewin in another. After they ate dinner in a restaurant and returned to the motel, Gewin and Massie went out shopping. Della was lying on the bed reading when she heard a knock on her door.

It was Floyd. Not having expected him to come to her room, she just cracked the door and asked him what he wanted. "Excuse me, Della Raye," he said politely. "Can I come in?" She opened the door.

Floyd sat down, looked around, and commented on her room and the fun they'd been having on the trip so far. She had known him only a short while, but she knew he had more on his mind than just small talk. Suddenly he grew serious, leaned forward, and gazed directly into her eyes.

"This Fred that you go out with," Floyd said. "What kind of a guy is he anyway?"

The question took her by surprise. "Oh, he's a pretty good guy," Della answered. "He takes me out fairly often. He treats me fine. We have fun."

"How is it between you and him?" Floyd asked. "Are you going steady with him, do you date others, or what?"

Surprised again by his directness, Della Raye answered, "As far as I'm concerned, Fred's just a friend. He might tell you different if you asked him, but that's the way I feel about it."

"Well, I've just been wondering about him," Floyd said. "That's what I wanted to know." And he left.

He was just checking out the competition. That's the way he was.

Della Raye enjoyed the weekend with Floyd, and for a while she dated both Fred and him without Fred's knowledge. Fred grew suspicious, however, and one night she spotted him following them behind Floyd's car. Fred phoned her the next morning and told her she had to make up her mind—it would be either Floyd or him, not both. That was the end of Fred.

Della Raye had been reading books constantly since she had taught herself to read. Most of them told of an ideal world: of good people and bad people with few in-betweens and obsessive loves that carried the heroes of the stories into ecstasies beyond their wildest dreams. She was intelligent enough to know that real life didn't work that way, but she had little experience to guide her.

She'd never known anyone like Floyd. She thought about him much of the time and couldn't understand why. He was a nice guy with a good sense of humor, but he often came across too stern and serious and bossy. He liked to dictate where they went on dates and everything they did. He clearly wanted to run the show, and Della Raye didn't like that. And when she voiced her own opinion, which she often did, Floyd didn't like that. They continued to see each other, and despite their differences, their relationship seemed to work.

They had been dating about four months when Floyd looked her dead in the eye and said, "Della Raye, I want to marry you. Will you marry me?"

"My Lord, Floyd," she said. "Doesn't this seem kind of quick? We haven't been going together all that long."

"I don't see that that makes any difference," he said. "I love you and I want to marry you. And I need your help raising my girls too."

"I don't know, Floyd," she said. "I've never been married and I've never been a mother. I have to think about this."

But Floyd wouldn't be put off for long. He kept reminding her of his proposal, and one evening shortly after he picked her up, he said, "Now Della Raye, we've got to get this thing settled. I want to marry you."

"Dang it, Floyd," she said. "I think I love you too, but it just seems like such a big step. And I need some time."

"Well, you need to make up your mind," he said. "I've got three girls at home, and I can't be spending all my time taking you to shows and stuff. We need to get married and get on with our lives."

Della mulled it over the rest of the evening, then gave him her answer: "All right, Floyd, I'll marry you. But I don't want to say when just yet."

Floyd nodded, a slight grin creasing his face and his gray eyes shining. He gave her an engagement ring, a sparkling little diamond set high on a plain gold ban, on their very next date. She knew he couldn't afford it.

"Oh, Floyd. It's so beautiful," Della Raye said as he slipped it on her finger. "You didn't need to do all that."

"Yes I did," he said.

Della looked at the diamond on her finger a thousand times a day. She felt tremendously happy and honored one moment, and afraid and overwhelmed the next. She was twenty-seven years old; Floyd was forty-four. He had all those girls, three of them still at home and one an invalid. And he knew nothing of her childhood.

Amy's shop was abuzz with the news. The other beauticians admired Della's ring, congratulated her, and made her show it to every customer. She enjoyed the attention, until one day as she was passing a picture of Floyd around the shop, a customer looked at it and said, "That's Floyd Hughes. I used to go out with him." Then the woman looked at her seriously and said, "I wouldn't marry him, Della Raye. I'd stay away from Floyd Hughes if I was you."

Della couldn't help thinking about what the customer had said, and that evening after work one of the other beauticians took her out to dinner and brought up the subject. Unbeknown to Della, the customer who had spoken disparagingly of Floyd had urged the beautician to try and talk her out of marrying him.

"Personally I don't know Floyd or anything about him," her friend said, "but that woman in the shop today was really serious when she talked about him. She said he's a tough guy, and he's got all those girls at home, Della Raye. And you're so young," the woman continued. "You don't know anything about raising a bunch of girls that age."

Della Raye couldn't argue. Those very concerns had been troubling her ever since she'd agreed to marry him. She worried every minute until she saw him again.

"Floyd," she said, "I don't think you want to marry me."

"Why not?" he asked.

"Because you just don't," she replied. Choking back tears, she pulled off the ring and held it out to him. He wouldn't take it.

"I'm not taking that ring," Floyd said. "It's yours. I gave it to you because I plan to marry you."

Della Raye broke down. "Floyd, you seem to think I'm some kind of great thing," she sobbed. "But you don't know anything about me."

"What don't I know about you?" he asked.

"You don't know a thing about me. Nothing about where I grew up, nothing about my family—nothing."

"Well then, tell me about those things," Floyd said.

"I grew up in Partlow. I lived with a bunch of idiots all my life. Nobody loved me when I was little. Nobody ever paid any attention to me, and I never got any education.

"They beat me all the time, abused me, and called me an imbecile. I can't even tell you some of the things they did to me," she said, her voice breaking, "because I can't stand to think of them myself.

"Nobody ever came to visit me or even wrote me a letter while I was growing up. I never felt like I was worth anything. I know how to read and write and how to fix hair, but that's about all."

Floyd listened quietly, his intense gray eyes softening as she talked.

"And family?" Della Raye said. "Yeah, I've got a family, in Partlow. My mother is in there, and my two brothers, or half brothers. I'm illegitimate, and so are they. I don't know who my father was or who their's was. My mother is simpleminded, and can't read or write. One of my brothers is retarded like my mother, and the other one is so crazy he can't even talk."

Della stopped, gathered her composure, looked into his eyes, and asked, "Is that the kind of family you want to marry into, Floyd?"

Floyd looked thoughtful for only a moment, then answered. "I don't want to marry your family, Della Raye. I want to marry you."

On December 22, 1951, three years after she was released from Partlow, Della Raye married Floyd Hughes.

Betty, the next-to-oldest married daughter, had children to keep her busy. Mildred, the oldest, whose husband was away in the military, had no children; so while Floyd and Della went on a short honeymoon, she stayed with the younger ones: Mary, seven; Sarah, nine; and Patsy, sixteen.

Della Raye had a task ahead of her with the girls; one so difficult it was probably just as well she had underestimated it. Her oldest stepdaughter was only three years younger than she, but Della was determined to become a mother to the girls. Determination had carried her through most of the battles in her life, but this was one battle for which Della Raye was unprepared. She didn't understand the rules, if there were any, nor did she realize that under the best of conditions stepparents often find themselves with two strikes against them from the start, maybe three. No matter how well-meaning stepparents may be or how determined they are to do the right thing, they are often seen simply as unwelcome replacements and encounter only resentment from their stepchildren.

Della Raye's stepdaughters had lost their mother early in life. Long before any such thing is ever supposed to happen, she had died and left them, an unfairness no child could be expected to understand. Then three years later their father brought home a new bride, a STEPMOTHER, who was not much older than them—far too young for the role and obviously inexperienced. And worse yet, this young stepmother had been in a mental institution.

To her stepdaughters, she would always be Della Raye, and because she was too young to be called Grandmother, Betty's children called her Raye-Raye. It would take years for any real closeness and understanding to develop between Della Raye and the girls, but her entire existence had been a battle. No matter how difficult life became, she carried on.

At times I felt like they were ashamed of me, and I can understand that now. There I was, trying to replace their mother and barely older than them, and from a mental institution as well. Years later I would think: how could I blame them for the way they had felt?

The five of them lived in a small rented house at first, and Della Raye continued to work at Amy's. Besides learning how to deal with a family, she was beginning to develop a good sense of business—an appreciation for the value of ownership and a nose for money. A few months after they were married, she and Floyd found a partially completed house for sale in Holt, an industrial suburb of Tuscaloosa. The house sat beyond the limits of current development on a remote street that ran along the crest of a hill overlooking the Black Warrior River. Having decided the location was too isolated for him, the man building it offered to sell them the house unfinished, along with an acre of land, for a thousand dollars.

Floyd had always been conservative with his money, but raising five girls, one of whom required multiple operations as she grew up, had taken all of it. Della Raye had a frugal nature as well, and despite her initial problems finding a job, she had managed to save more than a thousand dollars. With her money they bought the house.

Della Raye awoke to a considerable surprise the first morning in their house. Exactly at six o'clock, the shrill sound of an all-too-familiar whistle drifted up the hill. Partlow was not visible from the house, and she hadn't realized that the institution lay only about three miles away. It was the very sound that had awakened her for twenty years.

"That's the Partlow whistle!" Della Raye exclaimed when the piercing sound came through their open window. Floyd looked at her in horror, but relaxed when Della lay back and laughed. "Oh my!" she said. "I guess I didn't get far enough away."

Floyd worked on the house every evening and weekend. He

finished it around them while Della Raye made dresses to sup-
plement their income. After completing the house, Floyd
installed a two-room beauty shop in one end. The fully-
equipped shop had its own entrance and a sign on the door that
proudly announced: Della's Beauty Shop. She was in business.

Because Della Raye had never learned to drive, Floyd
always took her to the grocery store. He didn't really seem to
mind, though; with his penchant for control, it enabled him
to keep a close eye on what she spent. Floyd would push the
cart while Della did the shopping, and sometimes after she
selected an item that he considered too expensive, he'd
sneak it back out of the cart and set it on a shelf. Although he
did this when he thought she wasn't looking, Della caught
him at it several times but never mentioned it.

Della had always used lard for baking, but she learned that
pies, cakes, and cookies were tastier when made with cooking
oil. She decided to buy a can of Crisco, but knowing that it
cost more than lard, she suspected that Floyd would try to
sneak it out of the basket behind her back. In order to accom-
plish the purchase, Della routed them through the grocery
store so that they passed by the shelf with the cooking oils last.
That way she knew Floyd wouldn't have a chance to remove
the Crisco before they reached the checkout lane.

It worked. Della Raye had her can of Crisco. Floyd said nothing,
just loaded the groceries into the trunk of the car and drove home
as always. There he unloaded the groceries and carried them into
the house while Della was putting them away. In the kitchen, however, she couldn't find her can of Crisco. Exasperated, she went
through all the bags a second time and looked in the pantry to see
if possibly she had already put it away. There was no Crisco.

Floyd was sitting in the living room by now, so Della Raye
casually walked out to the car and lifted the trunk lid. Tucked
away in a corner of the trunk, wrapped inside a rag, lay the
can of Crisco. Leaving the Crisco there, she closed the trunk
and said nothing. Floyd returned it and got the refund.

But that was only a skirmish; the great "Battle of the Crisco" had just begun. The next time they went grocery shopping, Della Raye walked by the cooking oil early in the game and picked up another can of it. Noting exactly where she placed the Crisco in the cart, she kept a watchful eye on it as they moved through the store.

Sure enough, a few minutes later Della Raye caught him setting the Crisco on a shelf. She turned on him. "What are you doing, Floyd?" she asked loudly. Floyd glanced around uncomfortably, and didn't have an answer. "I want to learn to make cakes and cookies and things like that," she said, raising her voice loud enough to be heard several aisles away.

"You don't need anything to cook with but lard," Floyd said, keeping his voice low. "You've always made cakes and cookies and everything else with lard. What's wrong with it now?"

"I mean I want to make good cakes and cookies," Della said, "and pies, and bread, and anything else I might want to bake."

She pointed at the can and said, in a voice that carried the length of the store, "I mean for you to put that Crisco back in this cart, Floyd. Now."

Floyd ducked his head and glanced furtively up and down the aisle. People were watching. "I'm going out to the car, Della Raye," he huffed under his breath. "You're embarrassing me."

"Then you'd better leave the money with me," she said, "because I plan to finish the shopping." Floyd handed her the money, walked straight out of the store without a glance to either side, and sat and waited in the car.

Because I was so young, he thought he could treat me like one of his girls. I'd take just so much of that, then I'd let him have it.

Although Floyd seemed to like driving Della Raye wherever she went, she wasn't so fond of the arrangement herself. She wanted to learn to drive. Floyd resisted, and for a while the situation remained the same—not exactly the same, however. Della worked on him constantly about teaching her how to drive. Finally one day she wore him down.

"Now, Floyd," she said for the five-hundredth time. "It's high time I learned to drive that car."

"Oh, Della Raye," he sighed. "Why in hell do you want to learn to do that?"

"So I can go to the grocery store by myself if I want to, go to visit folks, drive to church, things like that," she said. "Now are you going to teach me how to drive that thing, Floyd, or am I going to have to just climb in it and take off by myself?"

"Oh, okay," he said, drawing a long breath. "We'll give it a try."

Floyd sat behind the wheel as Della Raye climbed into the passenger seat beside him. "Now you watch everything I do," he said. She nodded intently.

They drove down side streets and through neighborhoods. Floyd instructed her all the way on how to operate the car's controls and explained traffic laws as well. He showed her several times how to start, stop, and maintain speed, then he drove to a little back road and told Della Raye it was her turn.

They traded places. Della gripped the wheel firmly, looked over the hood and down the road with determination, pushed in the clutch, threw the car in gear, stepped on the accelerator, and took off with a terrible jerk. Floyd grabbed the dash to steady himself, a scowl creasing his face. "Remember what I told you now," he cautioned.

"I remember," she said.

"That's not how I showed you to do that, Della Raye."

"Yes it is."

"It won't work that way, Della Raye."

"Well, that's just the way you told me to do it, Floyd."

"No it's not. Hey, be careful! You're gonna wreck us."

"Oh, I am not. I'm just doing what you told me to do."

Somehow they managed to finish the ordeal alive, but the driving lessons were clearly not going to work. Floyd refused to ride with her again, but Della was undaunted. She asked Margaret, a regular customer and friend of hers, to ride along while she practiced driving. She didn't tell Floyd her plan, but the next time Margaret came to the house, Della confronted him.

"Floyd, Margaret said she'd ride with me and help me learn to drive."

Floyd looked up from his chair, shook his head, and handed her the keys. "All right," he said disgustedly. "But I figured Margaret had better sense than that."

"I'll be real careful," Della said, bounding out the door with the keys in her hand. Floyd stood on the step and watched them drive away. The car jerked, roared, veered, and bounced out of sight as Della fought a losing battle to coordinate the clutch, brake, accelerator, and steering wheel. Floyd sighed and walked back in the house.

A short while later Floyd heard the car roaring back toward the house. He stepped out onto the porch and stood with his hands on his hips, watching the tortured progress of his car jerking down the street. Gripping the wheel like doomsday, Della glanced over at him, attempted a little wave, and ran off the road and up the side of a high dirt bank. Floyd shook his head and retreated back into the house.

Margaret bravely returned for more lessons, and Della Raye slowly improved. Then one day as Floyd was leaving for work, she said, "Mildred's coming over today and taking me to get my driver's license."

"You're going to take a driving test?" he asked.

"Yes, I am," she said defensively. Floyd grunted and left.

When he walked in that evening, Della Raye proudly waved her license in the air. "I got it," she said.

"They gave you a driver's license?" Floyd asked incredulously.

"Yes, they did," Della replied. "I passed everything."

"What about the part where they ask if you've been in a mental institution?" he said.

"You don't think I was dumb enough to fill out that part, do you?" she said.

Della Raye joined the Holt Baptist Church soon after they bought their house, and quickly became an active member.

At about the same time she joined the church, she discovered she was pregnant. Feeling the life growing in her body brought her immense joy, but her family history worried her greatly. Her mother was feebleminded, though not to a great degree, and she had no idea who her father was. She did feel reasonably certain that he was not the same man who had fathered her brothers, and for that she was thankful.

Why did Della Raye choose to have children when she herself had doubts about the genetic factor? Because she loved children, and like millions of other people, she wanted a family of her own. And she believed that she had as much right to a life as anyone else. She had always believed that.

As with the rest of her life, Della Raye placed her baby in God's hands. She went to church often, read the Bible, and prayed every day that it would be normal. And through it all she had Floyd's unfailing support. He was happy about the baby, and never voiced a single misgiving or fear during her pregnancy.

Donny Raye Hughes was born November 23, 1952—seven pounds, four ounces of handsome baby boy. Donny would grow to be a husky picture of his father, cheerful like his mother, talkative like both of them, and exceptionally bright.

Floyd Jr., a second boy who would forever be known as Butch, was born three years later. Butch was also bright, but he proved to be the quiet one. With his customary wry grin, Butch says that growing up with three others who talked all the time made it difficult to get something said anyway.

With five children at home and a beauty shop to run, Della Raye kept a busy schedule. It seemed to come second nature to her; due to the strict regimentation in which she had grown up, she ran everything in her life that way. But since she never discussed her childhood with the children, they could not understand why she ran the house on such a tight schedule and with such strict discipline.

Donny Hughes smiles when he speaks of his childhood, his eyes dancing like his mother's. And like his father, he tells it straight. "When it came time for lights out at night, every light in that house had better be out. And when Mama told you it was time to get up in the morning, you might get away with letting her call you a second time, but you'd better not try a third."

"And if she had a chore for you to do," Donny continues, "you might as well do it right then and get it over with, because she wouldn't leave you alone until it was done."

The children knew their friends' houses weren't run with the discipline of an army barracks, and at times the strictness and regimentation bothered them. It scared them when their mother had nightmares too. Della Raye's nightmares were always the same: some fearsome, faceless person was trying to chase her down. And just before the person caught up with her, she always woke up screaming.

Floyd would take the children aside and try to explain. "Your mother has been through a lot that you don't know about," he'd tell them. "I don't even know everything about it myself. I know it's hard for you to understand, but she loves you, and she's doing the best she can."

"She called us 'honey,' 'darling,' and things like that all the time," Donny says fondly. "We knew Mama loved us, and she was doing the best she could. She may have been different from other mothers when we were growing up, but Mama was learning; and every year she got better."

Della Raye's children and stepchildren may have disagreed with her strict ways, but they never had to wonder whose side she was on.

A few years after Floyd and Della bought their house, Floyd's daughter Betty and her husband built a house next door to them. Several relatives from Floyd's side of the family gathered at Betty's place one holiday, including his daughter Mildred who was pregnant. A cousin from out of town lost her temper and tried to start a fight with Mildred in Betty's house; and though Della Raye bristled at the woman's remarks, because she was not blood relation to that side of the family she was determined to stay out of the quarrel. She left and walked back to her own house, and was sitting reading a book when Donny burst through the door a few minutes later.

"Mama!" Donny cried. "That woman's threatening to hit Mildred. I'm afraid she's gonna hurt her!"

Della Raye jumped up and raced back to Betty's house. The woman was leaning directly into Mildred's face when Della came through the door. "Hey!" Della said, pointing a threatening finger and striding purposefully across the room. "What do you think you're doing, treating this girl like a dog?"

The woman turned and looked warily into Della's face, now inches from hers. "This girl is pregnant," Della said through clenched teeth. "Can't you see that?" The woman didn't answer.

"You've been determined to have a fight all day long," Della continued evenly. "Well, if that's what you want, you've got one. Just follow me outside, and we'll get it on."

The woman broke from Della's glare and looked fearfully around the room for support. Finding none, she backed away.

"Come on, Mildred," Della said. "Let's go to my house."

Patsy's arthritis attacked her at the age of five, stunted her growth, and slowly but steadily crippled every joint in her body. Her diminutive frame would require nine surgeries before she was grown. At one point she had to learn to walk again. The rheumatoid could not destroy her positive outlook, however, or her radiant smile. In spite of it all, Patsy remained a cheery, spirited girl determined to live the best life she could.

Patsy possessed a brilliant mind, and dreamed of becoming a teacher. After finishing high school, she enrolled in the state university at Montevallo, a town thirty-five miles from Tuscaloosa. She lived in a dormitory at the college, and though she could barely walk unaided and suffered constant pain, she studied day and night, determined to earn a degree. Della loved Patsy's spirit, and encouraged her to never give up.

Patsy didn't give up, but during her senior year, the strong medication she was taking to combat the pain began to affect her nerves and trouble her sleep. Her rigorous study habits would not be compromised; since she couldn't sleep she studied even harder. Along with her obsessive work habits, the chronic insomnia took its toll.

Floyd and Della received an urgent call from a school official one morning, telling them that Pasty seemed abnormally weak and mentally disoriented. They drove to Montevallo immediately.

Besides appearing drawn and weak, Patsy seemed strangely distracted, out of contact with her surroundings. Despite her strong protests to remain at school, Floyd and Della took her home. During the drive to Tuscaloosa, Patsy's mind wandered. They listened quietly as she talked of imagined tortures the people at the college had put her through and described other wild fantasies as well. She calmed considerably when she went to bed that evening, but sometime after midnight Della heard a noise and got up to check. Patsy was nowhere in the house. Della found her standing in the carport clad only in her nightgown.

Della approached her quietly. "What are you doing out here, Patsy?" she asked. For a moment, Patsy didn't seem to comprehend, then she turned, looked around, and broke into tears.

"I don't know what I'm doing out here, Della Raye," she sobbed. "And I don't know what's wrong with me either."

"Come on back inside," Della said, reaching an arm around her shoulders and leading her into the house. "You can get in bed with us. Maybe you can go to sleep there."

Patsy stopped, and shook off Della's arm. "No," she protested. "I'm grown. I'm in college. I'm too big to be sleeping with you and Dad."

"But you can't sleep," Della said. "And I won't be able to either if I don't know where you are." Patsy reluctantly climbed into Floyd and Della's bed and lay down between them.

The following morning Patsy told Della to call Mildred. "I want to talk to my sister," she said. Mildred came immediately, took one look at her younger sister and said she needed to see a doctor. When Della Raye nodded her agreement, Patsy told her to call him.

The doctor spent some time examining Patsy alone that afternoon, then he brought her out and talked to Della Raye, Floyd, and Mildred as well. He told them Patsy had had a nervous breakdown, and that she needed rest and professional treatment.

"This girl needs to be admitted to Bryce Hospital for a stay," the doctor told them. "Bryce is the only place she can get the kind of treatment she needs."

Della Raye looked at Floyd and put an arm around Patsy. "We'll have to talk this over among ourselves, doctor," she said, and led Patsy out the door.

Back at their house, Della protested the idea. "They won't do anything for her at Bryce," she told Floyd. "She'll just be there, and they'll never let her out. I just won't have her going there." Floyd didn't argue.

Patsy voiced fears of being alone at night, so Della Raye moved a cot into the girl's bedroom and placed it beside her bed. "You go ahead and sleep, Patsy," she told her. "I'll be close by." She slept in the same room with Patsy for three months.

Patsy slept, ate the big meals that Della cooked for her, and slowly gained back her strength and emotional stability. Sometimes in the night she'd wake up and ask fearfully, "Della Raye, are you there?"

"Yes, I'm here, honey," would come the comforting reply, and Patsy would go back to sleep.

The day finally came when Patsy told her she was ready to try it alone. "Just get me a little night light," she said, "and I think I can do it."

And so Patsy rejoined the world. A few weeks later she went to live with her sister Mary. Unfortunately, she wasn't able to finish college, but she didn't go to Bryce either.

Although Della remained reticent about her Partlow experience, she began to bring her mother to their house for holiday visits. She didn't clearly understand her own reasoning in bringing Ruby to their home; but the broad chasm that had grown between them during her childhood continued to close, albeit slowly; and perhaps, in some small way the visits helped to heal the deep emotional wounds that Della carried inside.

I don't know if I really loved my mother at that point or not. I brought her to the house for visits, but in ways I think I considered it more of a duty than anything else.

One aspect of Ruby's visits bothered Della greatly. In the evening when she took her back to Partlow and told her goodbye, her mother would reach out and try to hug her. The gesture was sincere, but being reminiscent of all the times that Ruby had tried to hug her after the childhood beatings, it repelled Della. When her mother reached out for her, Della Raye would reel back and leave her standing. However, many years later, Della Raye would be able to cross a final emotional bridge: she would hug her mother.

Floyd came to know Ruby during her visits, and he didn't seem bothered by her simple ways. In fact, it made him curious about the rest of Della Raye's family and the environment in which she had grown up. He went to visit Partlow and became acquainted with her Aunt Dovie, then he visited the Boys Colony and met Frank and Dickie Jr. as well. Following that, he wanted to meet Della's relatives in northern Alabama; and though Della didn't particularly care to see them herself, one weekend she and Floyd drove to Athens and visited Uncle Richard and his family for a few hours. He would never establish close relationships with them, but to his credit, Floyd showed a genuine interest in meeting what family Della had.

Floyd's father had been a Baptist preacher, but for unknown reasons he refused to go to church with Della Raye for several years after they were married. Finally he acquiesced, however, and began attending services regularly. Then one day to Della's surprise, Floyd vowed to rededicate his life to Christianity. She was beaming on the way home from the church service, but Floyd tried to temper her elation. "Now just because I've rededicated my life doesn't mean I'm going to be in that church every time the doors open, Della Raye," he said. "Why, you're there more than the preacher is."

"You just use your own judgment," she said, laughing. "I know what I'm going to do."

Floyd loved to take Butch and Donny hunting and fishing, but for years Della insisted the boys go to church every Sunday, regardless of what outdoor sport it got in the way of. Then one Saturday Floyd told them to get their gear ready to go fishing with him early the next morning.

The boys couldn't imagine how their mother would possibly allow such a thing on a Sunday, but they didn't question it; they just gathered up their fishing gear and hoped it was really going to happen. Early the next morning, about four o'clock, Floyd woke them. He loaded their gear into the pickup truck and headed for their favorite fishing spot. About halfway there, he pulled off to the side of the road and stopped.

It was pitch-black outside, the dampest, stillest, darkest time of the morning. As Butch and Donny looked at their dad quizzically, Floyd took off his hat and held it in his lap. "We're going to have a little prayer meeting here boys," he said. "Y'all bow your heads." And sitting side by side in the dim glow of the dash lights, Floyd led them in prayer. He ended by asking the Lord to please let the fish bite that day, then put his hat back on his head, grinned at the boys, and drove away.

Then they knew how their dad had managed to bargain Della Raye into letting him take them fishing.

Brother Elmore, the church pastor, asked Della Raye to read a prayer aloud in Sunday school one morning. To the minister's surprise, she looked at him uncomfortably then dropped her eyes and said nothing. Floyd cast a quick glance at her and read the passage aloud himself.

Later that morning Brother Elmore came to her with a question in his eyes. Della tried to explain. "I'm sorry about my reaction when you asked me to read the prayer, Brother Elmore," she said. "It goes back to something that happened when I was a little girl. While I was reciting the Lord's Prayer, another patient started making fun of me, and I've never been able to pray in public since."

"Another patient?" Brother Elmore asked.

"Yes," Della said, "a patient in Partlow, where I grew up."

Brother Elmore was dumfounded. Like most of his congregation, he hadn't known. But Della Raye trusted the man implicitly, and she felt a terrible need to tell someone about her childhood—to finally give voice to the trauma, the pain, and the anger locked inside her. Brother Elmore listened incredulously to the horrible memories that haunted her, and promised he would pray for her. She felt relieved just having shared it with him.

Della Raye's story astounded Brother Elmore, but he honored her confidence. He carried her secret to the grave.

CHAPTER ELEVEN

To Err Is Human

Beginning in about 1950, the year after Della Raye's release, the deplorable conditions within Partlow, and similar institutions across the country, came under public scrutiny. In a wave of publicity that was long overdue, an unsuspecting society would learn what crowded pigsties their mental institutions had become.

A Special Joint Legislative Committee was formed to investigate the operation and administration of Bryce Hospital and Partlow State School and to formulate a report on the living conditions within the institutions. In its official report, dated September 11, 1951, the Committee stated the following findings: Patients were not receiving periodic medical exams; the investigation found that some had not been examined for several years. The staff physicians acted primarily as business managers, and had no way of knowing whether a patient was improving or deteriorating, unless they could tell at a glance as they passed through the ward. Regular staff meetings were not being held to discuss care, diagnosis, or treatment of patients, and medical records were poor and incomplete. The buildings, having had little or no preventive maintenance, had deteriorated to a point that threatened the safety of the patients. The employees took no pride in their jobs, and with no recognition for their work and no central gathering place such as an employee lounge, they had no incentive to develop any pride. And, as the Legislative Committee stressed in its report, the greatest deficiency found was a lack of competent staff.

Newspapers across Alabama took up the cause, their incisive articles and candid photographs revealing horrors beyond what the public could imagine: a disheveled teenage girl with her wrists lashed to the arms of a chair, bending her head down and attempting to gnaw through the bindings with her teeth; small children with hopeless stares, their shirt sleeves knotted over their hands to prevent them from picking at their own bodies; patients badly disfigured from self-inflicted scars; a boy who'd spent endless hours pounding his head on a concrete floor.

During an interview with the *Montgomery Examiner,* R. C. Partlow introduced the reporter to a retarded girl who had recently lost four fingers on one hand. While working at the laundry, the girl had caught her hand in a steam ironer and burned it so badly that the fingers had to be amputated. In citing this disfiguring accident, Dr. Partlow stressed how the public needed to know the conditions under which the institution was forced to operate.

In 1952 Alabama ranked forty-third out of the forty-eight states in per capita expenditure for care of its mentally handicapped; yet despite all the media attention directed at the conditions within its institutions and protestations of outrage by its politicians, the state was not yet prepared to part with the tax dollars needed for improvements. The patient population continued to rise, and funding remained low.

A reporter touring Partlow in 1955 wrote: "In the violent ward in an Alabama hospital for the insane, women lie about on the floor, on their stomachs or on their backs, yelling and gibbering. Others perch atop benches like old hens to roost. The fire in some of their eyes is too bright and in the eyes of others the fire has gone out. Still others pound on doors, scream, or must be bodily restrained by attendants from harming themselves or others."

A 1957 editorial in the *Montgomery Advertiser Journal* read: "Pathos Everywhere Behind Walls of Partlow". The *Tuscaloosa News* ran pictures of attendants laying mattresses down the center aisles of wards to accommodate the overflow of patients. Day rooms, previously used for patient recreation and socializing, had become nothing but a sea of beds.

In 1957 Partlow had sixteen hundred patients living in spaces designed for eleven hundred; by the following year the population had grown to seventeen hundred. Struggling under conditions described by an eyewitness reporter as "dangerously overcrowded," Dr. Partlow had only one full-time medical assistant on his staff, one registered nurse, and one attendant for every fifty patients.

However late the message had been in coming, the relentless media coverage finally began making inroads to public consciousness. Long content to disregard the plight of its least fortunate, a staid society slowly turned its head to look, and grew sick at what it saw.

In December of 1958, the Alabama legislature appropriated two million dollars for new buildings at Partlow and Bryce. A bold headline in the *Birmingham News* stated: "Alabama's Shame To Become Alabama's Pride". But while the move was certainly a step in the right direction, the two million dollars proved to be a classic case of too little too late. A long period of trying years lay ahead before Partlow would become Alabama's pride.

Della Raye had much to be thankful for and much to be proud of. Most of her family and friends, those still alive, remained prisoners at Partlow. Many had died there and many more would in the future, but she had beaten the system. She had survived for twenty years, two decades that spanned one of the darkest periods in the history of mental health. And as she had struggled to grow up, the attendants strove mightily to break her will, but never could. She had fought them every day and risen above it all, maintained her dignity and self worth in a hellish place nearly devoid of both. Then after gaining her freedom, she had triumphed over yet another set of impossible odds and built a life for herself.

Della Raye recognized her good fortune, and thanked God often for helping her through her trials. But somehow her prayers of thanks seemed shallow; no matter how fervent she tried to make them or how often she repeated them, in her mind they rung hollow. For inside Della Raye dwelt a demon—anger—a terrible, consuming anger.

Why her? Why had she been singled out while other children had grown up with parents who loved them? Why had she had to fight every moment from the time she could remember just to remain human? She had always known she wasn't retarded, and the people at Partlow had known it too. She'd been only a child, yet they had tormented her, humiliated her, and tried to beat her into submission. And then when she got out, naive and terrified, others had tried to use her and exploit her to their own advantage.

Della Raye carried a heavy load. Although she strove mightily not to let her anger rule her life or affect the way she treated others, she dwelt long and bitterly on the past. She could never retrieve the priceless years she had lost. They had stolen her childhood and made her ashamed to speak of it, and she hated them for it. She hated them. She hated them. She hated them.

But at the same time that Della Raye was cursing her tormentors, she began cursing herself as well. She came to the realization that she loathed her own attitude, and in the depths of her bitterness, she discovered that she hated something else even more than she hated her former captors. She hated the hate.

In her heart Della Raye loved life and she loved people—most of them anyway. She had been feeling her bitterness growing, and could see nothing ahead but wasted years—a wasted life—unless she could somehow rid herself of the overpowering anger. But how, Lord? How could one possibly exorcise such a horrible demon as hate?

God told her the answer, gently but firmly: forgiveness. She would have to forgive.

Della Raye had known the answer before she began to pray, but simply hadn't been able to face it. And knowing it beyond a doubt did not ease her burden. Why Lord? After all I've had to endure, must I now endure this as well? She knew the answer to that too.

But how, Lord? How to forgive when everything inside her cried out to cling to the hatred? Hatred was easy—all one had to do was leave it untended, let it seethe and boil and poison its own container.

Forgiving? That seemed impossible. She prayed.

Being a thinking, reasoning person who always strove to consider every detail, Della Raye tried to place herself in the shoes of the attendants, to see the circumstances of her growing up from their viewpoint. At this point in her life, she realized what a terrible job the attendants had had. Uneducated, untrained, and laboring under horribly overcrowded conditions, they had been charged with a near impossible task. Forced to work long hours with little pay at a dirty, thankless job with no recognition, the attendants had been unhappy people who were not even allowed control of their personal lives. After twelve hours on their feet trying to clean too many patients who had fouled themselves and being inundated all the while by an unceasing litany of babbling, moaning, and screaming—attempting in vain to ride herd on a milling mob incapable of reason—wouldn't the patience of most people likely have run a little thin?

Such a task would try the patience of anyone, of course, but Della Raye had worked harder than most of the attendants and lived in the same maddening crowd not twelve but twenty-four hours a day. She may have been a compassionate person, but when Della compared the lives of the Partlow attendants to her own she could find no room for sympathy.

And aside from the comparison and all the logic, what the real question came down to was simple: could the employees be excused for abusing patients, for trying to break the spirit of a little girl in order to brush her aside, push her off into the murmuring crowd of hollow-eyed souls who had given up hope so she would be out of their way?

No. Della Raye could never accept that. No human, under any circumstance, had the right to degrade another.

From whatever vantage point one chose to view her child-hood, the Partlow people had not done right. But however great those past injustices may have been, Della Raye could not allow herself to dwell on them. Down that road lay spite and vindictiveness—the bitter, angry masks of self-pity. For-giving must be forgiving—unconditional and absolute.

Della Raye had no idea how to go about climbing the Mount Everest of forgiving, so for the time being she let it rest and prayed for the strength to do whatever it was that she had to do. She didn't yet know the way, but she trusted God to help her find it.

The phone rang one summer evening in 1962. "Della Raye?" a half-familiar voice asked when she picked it up.

"Yes, this is Della Raye," she said.

"This is your Uncle Richard, Della," the voice on the other end said hesitantly.

She gripped the phone like a vise, and found herself unable to speak.

Richard went on. "Me and Bonnie was thinking about comin' down there to visit you and Floyd for a few days," he said, "if that'd be all right."

Finding her voice with difficulty, Della managed a reply. "Well, Uncle Richard, this sure is a surprise."

"Bonny's sixteen now; I know you'd like her," Richard said. "And we sure liked Floyd when y'all come up here to see us that time," he continued. "You didn't do much talkin' your-self, and you didn't stay very long, but I guess I can under-stand that."

Della thought for a moment, then answered. "Okay, Uncle Richard, we'll be looking for you."

"We'll be down on the bus tomorrow evening," he said, and hung up.

A life of hard labor in the fields had dragged Richard's shoulders down into a permanent stoop, but other than that he looked like a fifty-some-year-old version of the lean, thin-faced, sloppily-dressed man he'd always been. The years had mellowed him a bit, though, and perhaps introduced him to morality; he smiled tentatively at Della Raye and seemed genuinely glad to see her.

Bonnie had become a lean stalk of corn, a homely teenager with a long, narrow face that unfortunately mirrored her father's, but her loving personality had survived. She grinned shyly and hugged Della as if she might remember that long-ago night when she had so proudly modeled the little dress that Della had sewn for her by hand. Driving home from the bus station, Della Raye eyed her faded cotton dress and vowed to take her shopping during their visit.

Della knew that Richard always awoke at four o'clock in the morning, farmer's hours; but while she was an early riser herself, four o'clock was just too much. As she was showing him to his bed she told him, "Now Richard, I want to ask you to do something while you're here—don't get out of this bed before five o'clock. We just don't get up that early around here."

Wasn't that ugly of me, making him do that? He was a farmer, and used to getting up earlier than we did. I know he just lay there awake in the mornings and waited until we got up.

One evening when Della Raye and Floyd were visiting with Richard in the back yard, sitting under the trees enjoying the calm remnants of twilight, he brought up the subject of Partlow. Sounding as if, perhaps, his conscience had finally caught up with him, Richard looked at her sorrowfully and said, "You may hate me for puttin' you in Partlow, Della Raye, but I knew that in there you'd at least lead a clean life, and that's what I wanted for you."

Della Raye was surprised at what he said, but not shocked. "What about that young couple who came to adopt me before you took me to Partlow?" she asked, pointedly but calmly. "Why wouldn't you let me go with them?"

"Why, there's no tellin' what might have happened to you if I'd let you go with them people," Richard said defensively. "As it is I know you've led a clean life, and besides that I didn't want to separate you from your mother."

"I didn't grow up with my mother," Della Raye told him, her voice still calm. "They took me away from her the day we got there. And I would too have led a clean life with that couple, and I could have been educated as well. I've always wondered what might have happened if I could have gone with them and been loved and got an education—what I might have become."

Richard stared at the ground. Floyd remained silent.

"And you're wrong about something else, Uncle Richard," Della Raye said. "I don't hate you."

Richard and Bonnie stayed for five days, and both seemed to enjoy the visit. As they prepared to board the bus for home, Della Raye found Richard looking at her awkwardly, shyly, and half-embarrassed, not knowing how to say goodbye. She reached out and gave him a hug, which he gratefully returned, and she waved to him as the bus pulled away. In the days following she thought of her uncle often, and relived their conversation about Partlow again and again. It seemed as though she had been talking to herself as well as him during the confrontation; and to her wonder, she realized it was true—she didn't hate him anymore.

Edna Coen, Partlow's imperious personnel manager who had enslaved Della Raye in her home, became a victim of early dementia, possibly Alzheimer's Disease. Though Edna was only in her fifties, in 1971 Della heard that she had been admitted to a nursing home.

Feeling sure that Edna wouldn't have many visitors, Della found herself thinking about the woman sitting there alone in the nursing home. To her own surprise, she considered going to visit Edna. Doubt filled her mind as she mulled it over; however, she had not seen the woman in years, and wondered if Edna would accept her and if she would accept Edna.

Finding no other answer except to take the chance, Della closed her shop the following Monday and drove off to visit Edna Coen. As she approached the nursing home, she became so emotionally overwhelmed that she would never be able to describe the moment nor even remember it clearly. She remembers sitting in her car gripping the steering wheel, afraid to open the door, afraid to move. Any other thing on earth would have been easier than this, but this she had to do.

The bitter woman with the scars crisscrossing her face was no longer the alert, efficient manager who had marched around the Administration Building barking orders and hiring and firing at will. Edna's stiffly erect body had lost its form; the stern face had fallen; and the fire in her piercing eyes had died. With a dull, quizzical stare, she sat and surveyed her surroundings, a shrinking world with which she was losing contact.

Edna looked around at Della's approach, and for a moment didn't recognize her. Then the confusion in her seamed face turned to a crooked smile and her eyes brightened a bit. "Why, Della Raye," she exclaimed.

"Hello Edna," Della said. "How are you?"

Edna spoke slowly, straining to find the words. "Oh, I guess I'm okay. How are you, Della?"

"I'm fine."

"I didn't expect to see you," Edna said.

"I don't guess I expected to see you either," Della replied.

Della sat down in a chair opposite hers and they talked awhile, then Edna asked, "Would you take me for a walk, Della Raye? I can go for walks if somebody takes me."

"Sure," Della said, and helped her to her feet.

Della held her by the arm and they walked slowly down the hall, talking as they went. Edna's awareness seemed to come and go, and it took all of her concentration to focus on a single thought. As they neared the front door, Edna pointed at it and asked Della to walk her outside.

"Oh, they told me you weren't supposed to go outside," Della said.

Suddenly Edna stiffened and jerked her arm away, her eyes snapping with defiance. "Dammit to hell!" she screamed, waving her arms wildly. "They won't let me do anything around here. You take me out that damn door, Della Raye. Now!"

"No, Edna," she answered calmly. "We can't do that."

Della stood still, and watched the rage pass as quickly as it had come. Within moments a visible change came over Edna: her stiffened posture relaxed; her face dropped, and her eyes went dull again.

Della stepped close and took her by the arm. "Come on, honey," she said. "Let's walk back down the hall."

They returned to Edna's room and Della Raye helped her into her chair. "There now, we had a nice walk, didn't we?" Della said.

"Yeah, we sure did," Edna replied, apparently with no memory of the fit of anger that had gripped her just minutes before. Then the impossible happened. Edna reached out, took her hand, and said, "I'm glad you came to see me, Della Raye."

Della squeezed her hand and touched her shoulder softly, her eyes brimming with tears. "I'm glad I came too, Edna. I'm so glad."

Della Raye went to visit Edna again the following Monday, and avoided the outside doors when she took her for another walk. She visited her the next Monday, too, and every week for the rest of Edna's life. When the woman's mind faded to a point that she could no longer recognize her, Della sat and held her hand to let her know that someone cared.

Betty Myers ended up in another nursing home. The tyrant of Partlow's kitchen had driven Della Raye unmercifully through her teen years, had her thrown into the Cross Hall, kicked her mother like a mongrel dog, and worked them both like beasts of burden. Now Myers was old and weak. She, too, would lose her mind before she died, but at this point she was still feisty and mean.

One Monday after she finished her visit with Edna Coen, Della went to see Betty Myers. Her old nemesis had always been thin, but wiry and strong. As Della Raye approached she could see her sitting limp and helpless in a wheelchair, her body deteriorated into little more than a bony frame.

Myers recognized her instantly. "What're you doin' here, Della Raye?" she asked in a caustic tone.

"I've been visiting Edna Coen," Della answered, "and thought I'd stop by and see how you're doing, Miss Myers."

"Oh hell, I suppose I'm doin' okay," Myers said. "I heard Edna's in a nursing home too. I reckon we'll all end up in one of these damn places eventually."

"Maybe so," Della said. "Anyway, I'm glad to see you, Miss Myers."

"I'm glad to see you too, Della Raye. You ain't got any snuff on you, do you?"

"No, I don't have any," Della said. "I don't use it."

They sat and visited for a few minutes, something Myers did poorly and was not particularly fond of; then Della Raye pushed her around the nursing home in her wheelchair. Della stopped to greet other patients and talked with them momentarily as they moved down the hall. Myers remained as haughty and socially inept as always; she nodded and spoke to her neighbors, but offered little else.

After they returned to Myers' room and Della Raye was leaving, she said, "I visit Edna every Monday, Miss Myers. I'd enjoy stopping by to see you if you'd like me to."

"Yeah, I'd like that Della Raye. And when you come next time, would you bring me some snuff?" she asked.

"Okay, I will," Della said. "I'll see you next Monday."

On her way out, a nurse stopped Della at the desk. "Did Miss Myers ask you to bring her some snuff?" the nurse asked.

"Why yes, she did," Della answered.

"Please don't bring her any," the nurse pleaded. "She has plenty of it, but she's so addicted to it that we have to keep it here at the nurses' station and ration it out to her a little at a time."

When Della came to visit Myers the following Monday, she immediately asked about the snuff. The cantankerous woman wasn't happy to learn that Della hadn't brought it, but after she cooled down she seemed glad for the company anyway.

Della Raye continued to visit Myers every Monday for several years. When the woman's mind began to drift away she talked about snuff constantly and demanded that Della bring it to her every week. Della smiled, wheeled her around the nursing home, and chatted with her neighbors until she passed away.

Only a handful of people attended the funeral when Betty Myers died. Della Raye was one of them. She kneeled and prayed for the woman's soul.

Madelyn Samuel, the woman who lay in bed wasted with cancer, had been surprised by Della's visit and even a little frightened. The domineering supervisor had made her sleep in a fouled bed at the age of five, ruthlessly ripped her new dress off her body as a teenager, and looked the other way while scores of attendants beat her brutally; but she seemed genuinely happy to see Della Raye in the hospital that day. And Della was happy to see Miss Samuel.

The cancer exacted its toll within a few days of Della's visit, and as Miss Samuel had predicted, she was not there the following Monday. Della Raye went to visit her nonetheless. At the funeral home she brushed, combed, and styled the woman's hair. It was the last thing she could do for her.

Miss Rule, the attendant whose keys Della Raye and Verna had stolen to make their getaway as teenagers, had nearly lost her job over the incident. When Della heard that Miss Rule had also been hospitalized with cancer, she feared the woman would not welcome a visit from her. One Monday she decided to brave it.

"I imagine you hate me," Della said, gingerly walking into Miss Rule's room.

The sick woman smiled wanly and touched her with a skeleton of a hand. "Oh, Della Raye, I could never hate you," she said.

"But we almost got you fired that time we tried to escape," Della said.

Miss Rule laughed weakly but merrily. "Yes, you did," she said. "But who could blame you? You didn't belong in that place, Della Raye. I knew there wasn't anything wrong with you, and a lot of other employees knew it too."

She laughed again. "I'd have tried to escape too if I'd been you."

Miss Rule complained of being cold in the hospital, so Della Raye crocheted a warm cape and brought it to her. The dying lady was delighted.

Della Raye continued to visit every Partlow attendant admitted to a hospital or nursing home—the kind ones, the indifferent ones, and the ones who had beaten her and forced her mother to beat her. She talked with them, laughed with them, prayed for them, and brought them things they needed as long as they lived. Some may never have understood why she went out of her way to brighten their lives, but Della Raye did.

You can not be a child of God if you hold hatred in your heart.

Epilogue

Floyd suffered a heart attack in 1988 at the age of eighty and fell dead in Butch's arms. Three of Floyd's daughters, Patsy, Mary, and Mildred, are also gone. Della Raye speaks warmly of her stepdaughters, living and deceased, and refers to them simply as "my girls."

Butch Hughes manages a large machine shop in Tuscaloosa and lives just down the street from Della Raye.

Donny Hughes, a middle-aged picture of his father with his mother's sense of humor, boundless energy, and quick intellect, became a successful businessman in Houston. The names of his two teenage sons appear on the honor roll every year.

Della Raye's grandchildren surprised her with a doll for Christmas when she was seventy-three, her first ever. She is one of the longest-standing members of Holt Baptist Church, and as Floyd laughingly accused her, continues to spend as much time there as the minister. And despite her protests that she hasn't enough education for the job, Della Raye gets elected president of her Sunday school class year after year, little wonder. How could a lady who has practically committed the Bible to memory not have enough education to teach Sunday school?

She still corresponds with several ex-Partlow patients, childhood friends who have lived their lives in shadows, in fear that their own families and friends might learn of their secret past.

Della Raye continues to live her life by strict routine and unrelenting punctuality. She prepares her own taxes each

227

year and sends them off a month before the deadline. Her Christmas shopping is finished by Thanksgiving, the packages wrapped and ready to go. She reads the Bible every day without fail; and each Monday morning she steps into her sporty red car and dashes off to brighten the lives of the old and infirm in Tuscaloosa's hospitals and nursing homes.

Her final stop is the nursing home where Massie lives. Badly stooped under a dowager's hump, Massie's posture now forces her to turn her pretty face to the side and upward to speak to someone; but at ninety she remains beautiful inside and out, the depth of her integrity reflected in the calm of her ageless eyes. Ruthless old age can neither invade the lady's serenity nor diminish Della's reverence for her.

After fifty years the nightmares still come, and Della Raye still screams herself awake. But on the wall of the bedroom, where she wakes from her subconscious panic, hang two needlepoint plaques. There is nothing in the world so strong as your belief in yourself, states one. The other depicts a little red engine chugging up a hill. I think I can, I know I can, it says.

An organization of senior citizens with whom Della tours once awarded her a cowbell, a tongue-in-cheek reference to her propensity for wandering away from the group and exploring on her own. On a recent trip to Tennessee, they were shopping and viewing exhibitions at a craft village that adjoined an amusement park. Never having the opportunity to visit such a place as a child, Della Raye slipped away from the others and went to try out the rides. The group eventually missed their wandering member, shook their heads, and went looking for her. An elderly lady pointed skyward and exclaimed, "There she is!"

They looked up and saw Della Raye waving merrily, high atop the Ferris wheel.

Appendix

The voices of reason tried to quell the relentless march of eugenics; unfortunately, their efforts ended in vain. Charles T. Wilbur, Superintendent of the Illinois Asylum for Feeble-minded Children, voiced his disapproval early in the movement, stating his views clearly in a 1909 letter to a fellow institutional director.

> "The ideas concerning the aims and objects for the institutions for the Feeble[-]minded are very different from what they formerly were. The whole aim of society is now to drive them into Colonies with very little effort as to their mental development.
>
> ". . . . The developing or ennobling influences of the Public Institution with the inmates kept in large classes of their own kind or worse are not for their own good. My views are decidedly changed since I learn that society only desires to get rid of them and be protected from them when the older ideas were to uplift them by every means that could be used. Now when thus congregated in droves like cattle it is about as much as we can accomplish to keep them comfortable and fed and clothed after a fashion, but without the affectionate influences most children get at home."
>
> "God help the defectives of the land," Wilbur concluded, "as man is failing to make much effort."

Wilbur's was not the only dissenting voice, nor by any means the most famous. H. H. Goddard—the nationally-acclaimed psychologist who had "discovered" the moron shortly after the turn of the century, bastardized Binet's IQ test to fit his own views, and delivered the first scientific paper on the subject of human eugenics—shocked his colleagues by publicly recanting his beliefs in 1928.

"It was for a time rather carelessly assumed that everybody who tested 12 years or less was feebleminded . . ." Goddard stated.

> "We now know, of course, that only a small percentage of the people who test 12 are actually feebleminded.
>
> "The problem of the moron is one of education and training. . . . I have no difficulty in concluding that when we get an education that is entirely right there will be no morons who cannot manage themselves and their affairs and compete in the struggle for existence.
>
> "Some will object that this plan neglects the eugenic aspect of the problem. In the community, these morons will marry and have children. And why not? . . . It may still be objected that moron parents are likely to have imbecile or idiot children.
>
> "There is not much evidence that this is the case. The danger is probably negligible. At least it is not likely to occur any oftener than it does in the general population."

"As for myself," Goddard concluded, "I think I have gone over to the enemy."

The most prestigious voice of eugenics, indeed the man accredited with the nationwide expansion of the movement, ultimately saw its folly; unfortunately, Goddard's enlightenment came too late. The gong had been rung too loudly, the runaway train sent speeding down the track long before he rethought his dangerous ideas. In an atmosphere that prompted the *Southern Medical Journal* to declare, "The new science of Eugenics is pregnant with great possibilities for the human race," the zealots had convinced legislators across the nation of the "Menace of the Feebleminded."

By 1922 nearly every Northern and Western state had established a separate institution for the feebleminded, a nationwide system of asylums that housed forty-five thousand patients. And although the Northern states pioneered the movement, the South quickly followed their lead. By

1923 similar institutions were founded in nine Southern states, including Alabama's Partlow. However, in their attempt to mimic the North, the Southern directors failed to account for the economic differences between the regions. The dire poverty set to descend on the South would prompt the Depression-era courts to turn the institutions into dumping grounds, not only for the feebleminded but also for orphans, degenerates, prostitutes, delinquents, and the aging poor as well.

Though feebleminded patients had undergone involuntary sterilization in many states by the turn of the century, by law the states had no such authority. Indiana was the first to formally enact a sterilization law in 1907. While some states resisted a practice they considered barbaric, most soon followed Indiana's lead. Despite protests, such as that of a Louisiana state representative who pleaded with his colleagues in open session, "I hope that the House will go on record as opposed to making slaughter houses out of our feebleminded asylums," and a South Carolina legislator's declaration that, "the state has no right to butcher its citizens," thirty-five states had enacted sterilization laws by 1935.

With the statutes in place, the states could and did sterilize the feebleminded against their will, along with degenerates, habitual criminals, the insane, and probably more than a few uneducated souls who simply found themselves in the wrong place at the wrong time.

Castration and ovariotomy were the preferred methods of some institutional directors, but public sentiment generally prevented the use of such radical measures. Vasectomy and salpingectomy, though still invasive procedures and the latter being especially dangerous for women, became the norm. Prior to 1900, however, a number of castrations did take place at the Kansas State Asylum for Idiotic and Imbecile Youth before a public outcry put a stop to the bloody practice.

Sterilizations peaked in the 1930s. Annually averaging twenty-five hundred nationwide but reaching nearly four thousand in one year, the practice began to diminish during the 1940s and 1950s. Not before sixty thousand U. S. citizens had been sterilized against their will did it finally end, however, with more than twenty thousand attributed to California alone. And though Alabama ceased the practice in 1935, sterilization would not come to a complete halt in the Deep South until the mid-1960s.

Two hundred and forty-four citizens of Alabama were sterilized prior to 1935, people whose only sin, in the impassioned words of the governor who stopped it, was having been born. And though Governor Graves' veto likely saved Della Raye from sterilization, W. D. Partlow would have done it differently if he could have. Even as allied armies were uncovering evidence of eugenics run wild in Nazi concentration camps, in 1945 Dr. Partlow and his colleagues mounted a final push to enact a sterilization law in Alabama. Della Raye was still a resident of Partlow at the time. She was twenty years old when a senate vote killed the bill.

W. D. Partlow never got the chance to try again. After thirty years as the number one man, the emphysema that would eventually take his life forced him to resign as Alabama's mental health director in 1949. Effective January 1, 1950, the system was placed under the direction of the newly-established State Department of Mental Health. R. C. Partlow, W. D.'s capable brother, directed Partlow for another fifteen years. A eugenicist who believed he was doing the right thing, R. C. retired in 1965 after fifty-three years of state service, twenty-one of them at Partlow. During his final years there, a deaf mute girl who had no family worked as a maid at his residence on the grounds. When Dr. Partlow and his wife left, they took the girl with them to ensure that she would have a home.

The great pseudoscience of eugenics, the would-be cure-all for the human race, left thousands of innocent lives destroyed in its wake. Unfortunately, the sixty thousand sterilized were not its only victims; countless more became institutionalized and remained so for life. Many of these should never have been there in the first place. Like penned-up cattle, they continued to mill the crowded wards long after the practice of sterilization became history.

In 1972, as the state mental health system continued to struggle under the burden of too many patients with too little funding, a landmark court case swept Alabama into the national spotlight. The tinder was sparked when Dr. Stonewall Stickney, Alabama State Commissioner of Mental Health, terminated ninety-nine employees of Bryce Hospital due to a lack of funding. A group of attorneys representing Ricky Wyatt, an inmate at Bryce, filed a class action suit in federal court against Commissioner Stickney and other state officials. In *Wyatt v. Stickney* the lawyers alleged that in terminating the employees the state had denied Wyatt and his fellow patients their constitutional right to treatment.

Curiously, though criminals had constitutional rights such as habeas corpus, prior to the Wyatt case mental patients had none. In a ruling that reverberated across the nation, the presiding judge in *Wyatt vs. Stickney* held that involuntarily committed patients had a "constitutional right to receive treatment as will give each of them a realistic opportunity to be cured or to improve his or her condition."

As the eyes of the nation focused on Alabama, the judge went on to formulate minimum standards for treatment—a formidable list of rules, which were expensive. Worried legislators across the country heard the words they feared the most: the states would be responsible not only for implementation of the standards but also for funding them.

The new standards would provide a quality of life heretofore unknown for mental patients. Adequate facilities and staffing would be required as well as complete patient records, prompt medical treatment, telephone rights, therapeutic work assignments, interaction with the opposite sex, religious worship, privacy, and dignity. And most importantly, all were to be provided under the least restrictive conditions possible.

No longer would patients be locked away and forgotten. The sweeping changes could hardly be implemented overnight, of course, but at last a new day was dawning, a dawn that promised treatment, care, and dignity to the least fortunate members of society.

Wyatt v. Stickney shook the mental health system of Alabama to its foundations. Knowing that a time limit would be imposed for compliance with the new standards, the Department of Mental Health candidly admitted that many of the residents of Bryce were not receiving treatment nor even in need of it and asked the court for sixty days to identify patients who did not belong in the hospital.

Implementing the changes proved to be an impossible task for the state. When the time limit ran out, the judge deemed the state efforts inadequate and took unprecedented action. He placed the entire mental health system of Alabama under the jurisdiction of the federal court.

Although the case had been filed in the name of a patient at Bryce, the ruling in *Wyatt v. Stickney* applied to Partlow as well. The institution where Della Raye grew up fell under federal control in 1972 and remained so for a period of fourteen years. When control was returned to the state in 1986, Partlow would finally emerge as Alabama's pride.

With each state being responsible for funding and implementing the newly-established standards, the great "emptying out" began. Similar to the institutions in Alabama, many others across the country were packed with patients. The eugenic concepts that started the whole mess had long since failed; but because the courts had continued to use the institutional system as a dumping ground for every form of degenerate, indigent, and social misfit, Partlow's patient population had grown to a seam-splitting twenty-three hundred. It could never comply with the federal standards with so many bodies crowding the wards. The patients had to go. What to do with an institution full of patients—twenty-three hundred souls who, either because of mental disability and/or institutional-ization, were incapable of caring for themselves?

The older, long-term residents, such as Della Raye's mother, were the simplest to deal with; they were released to nursing homes. At the age of seventy-three, Ruby was trans-ferred to a nursing home in Collinsville, a small town in northern Alabama. Financial aid from the state's Department of Pensions and Security (Old Age Pension) covered her expenses until her death.

The younger and more helpless patients presented a greater problem. Though many would remain in Partlow, Dickie Jr. was transferred to a state facility in Powell, Alabama, where he lived until he passed away in his mid-sixties. Although Frank was incapable of existing on his own, being compliant and well-behaved, he qualified for Aid to the Permanently and Totally Disabled, a government program that would pay for his care outside of Partlow. With his beloved job at the Boys Colony gone, Frank wanted to be with his mother. In 1974, at the age of fifty-six, he was also accepted into the Collinsville nursing home where he and Ruby lived out their lives and were regu-larly visited by Della Raye, Butch, and Donny.

A third group of patients suffered arguably more than the aged and mentally disabled. It was the wrongly committed—the mildly retarded, eccentric, and normal—those who, like Della Raye, had never belonged there in the first place. Being more like frightened children than adults, painfully shy and lacking even the crudest social skills, they had never made a single deci-sion on their own. A harsh world awaited them outside the gate.

Partlow provided job coaches to assist the patients in obtaining employment, but they had virtually no skills to offer. Some did get menial jobs such as washing dishes and scrubbing floors in restaurants, and cleaning and changing beds in rest homes. Their employers, many of whom would hire them only on a trial basis, often took advantage of them. Six of Della Raye's old friends found work at a busy restau-rant, while still living at Partlow. They walked several miles to the restaurant each day to work a twelve-hour shift, a task for which the owner paid them a whopping six dollars per day. When Della heard of this travesty, she went looking for the restaurant owner and reviled him, but he was only one of many who exploited the ex-patients.

Along with her Aunt Dovie, Della Raye's childhood friends Grace and Mary died in Partlow a few years after her release. Aunt Dovie was sixty-four; however, Grace and Mary, who had spent nearly all their short lives in Partlow, were not yet thirty. All were buried in pauper's graves on the grounds of the institution. Although each of the three had been diagnosed with tuberculosis, an attendant secretly told Della's mother that Dovie had died of breast cancer. The truth may never be known, but Dovie's medical record does document a long-running open sore on one of her breasts, a sore that would never heal and was still being treated at the time of her death.

Lula Clemons, Willa Mae Kilpatrick, and Lorita Fricard, all middle-aged or beyond, found work at a local nursing home. The flirtatious Lorita never changed, nor did the comical bent of her life. Her swishing gait and roving eye caught the attention of a naive preacher who was visiting at the home where she worked. Lorita ended up marrying the wide-eyed fellow.

Willa Mae worked and lived as best she could but never found anyone with whom to share her life. Mercifully, a Tuscaloosa church took her under its wing; she lived as a ward of the church and the state until her death.

Lula worked at menial jobs and lived in subsidized housing but never lost the faith or the sense of humor that enabled her to weather a lifetime in Partlow. Lula was situated in a decent retirement home in her later years and proved resourceful to the end. After she became too weak to manage for herself, she petitioned Partlow to release her favorite niece so the young woman could live with her and care for her during her declining years. The niece was mildly retarded but a hard worker who had a loving nature. When Partlow refused Lula's request, she was undeterred. She wrote to Alabama's famous governor,

George Wallace, and asked him to intervene. Wallace did, and Partlow released Lula's niece. This from a woman who had been classified most of her life as mentally incompetent.

Lula went another step to preserve a modicum of dignity for herself and her relatives who had resided in Partlow. Somehow she managed to save enough money to purchase cemetery plots for her entire family, so that they wouldn't be buried in pauper's graves. Lula also bought a plot for Willa Mae, but her lonely friend didn't need it. The church folk who helped support Willa Mae laid her to rest in their cemetery. The sickly baby who had been abandoned on the steps of a church a lifetime before found her peace at last in the soil of another churchyard.

When Della Raye's Partlow friends came to her beauty shop, she fixed their hair for free; and when they grew too old to come to her, she went to them.

In 1962 the institution was renamed the Partlow State School and Hospital, and in 1989 gained its present name, the William D. Partlow Developmental Center. The Partlow of today is unrecognizable as the Partlow of old.

In the fiscal year of 1970-71, prior to *Wyatt v. Stickney,* Partlow's total operating budget amounted to approximately $5.5 million. By 1980-81, it had grown to $25.5 million. Partlow now boasts modern buildings, a highly-trained staff, and up-to-date facilities where residents receive personal care, treatment, affection, and more. Camp Partlow, a recreational area outside of town, offers activities such as boating, picnicking, and hiking, while the Lurleen Wallace Chapel on the grounds provides the residents easy access to their own house of worship.

The residents of Partlow, no longer known as idiots, imbeciles, morons, or inmates, live in a world free of locked doors and barbed wire fences—a caring atmosphere in which they are afforded the opportunity to overcome their handicaps to the greatest degree possible and to live life to their fullest potential, with dignity.

Bibliography

Frankl, Victor. *Man's Search for Meaning.* Pocket Books Division of Simon and Schuster, 1959,1962,1984.

Gould, Stephen Jay. *The Mismeasure of Man.* W. W. Norton and Company, 1981, 1996.

Grob, Gerald. *The Mad Among Us: A History of the Care of America's Mentally Ill.* Harvard University Press, 1994.

Larson, Edward. *Sex, Race, and Science: Eugenics in the Deep South.* Johns Hopkins University Press, 1996.

Larson, Edward., and Leonard Nelson, "Involuntary Sexual Sterilization of Incompetents in Alabama: Past, Present, and Future," *Alabama Law Review* 33, no. 2, (1992).

Noll, Steven. *Feeble-Minded in Our Midst: Institutions For the Mentally Retarded in the South, 1900-1940.* University of North Carolina Press, 1995.

Trent, James. *Inventing the Feeble Mind: A History of Mental Retardation in the United States.* University of California Press, 1994.

Hoole Special Collections Library. *Annual Reports, Partlow State School and Hospital.* Hoole Special Collections Library. Tuscaloosa:University of Alabama.

—. *Rufus C. Partlow Personal Scrapbook.* Hoole Special Collections Library. Tuscaloosa: University of Alabama.

Partlow Perspective. Vol. 10, no. 3, (Winter 1989-90).

William D. Partlow Developmental Center. Patient Records of Della Raye Rogers, Ruby Rogers, Dovie Rogers, Frank Rogers, Dick Rogers. William D. Partlow Developmental Center. Tuscaloosa, Alabama.